VICTORIAN
DOMESTIC ARCHITECT

A facsimile of Oliver P. Smith's

THE DOMESTIC ARCHITECT

*A Victorian Stylebook of 1854 featuring Rural and
Ornamental Cottages in Grecian and Cottage Styles*

*The American Life Foundation
Library of Victorian Culture*

1978

Production notes: This new edition was seen through the press by Walnut Grove Graphics and Book Production Associates in Watkins Glen, NY. Printing and binding was performed by Valley Offset, Inc. in Deposit, NY.

ISBN: 0-89257-042-3

THE DOMESTIC ARCHITECT by Oliver P. Smith is a curious Victorian amalgam of the plain, the fancy, and the exotic; Greek Revival houses, Downingesque cottages, and Italianate villas; practical advice, technology, lessons in architectural drawing, and two glossaries of terms. Architectural historians will instantly recognize it for what the trade calls *a transitional piece*—it is part "builder's guide" (popular in the late eighteenth and early nineteenth centuries) and part "stylebook" (popularized by A. J. Downing in the 1840s).

In addition to its considerable interest to architectural historians, what also recommended it to us for reprinting was its place of publication. During the decade of the 1850s, Buffalo, New York was an architectural book publishing center. Buffalo's building boom of the 1850s encouraged the publication in Buffalo of an edition of William Brown's *The Carpenter's Assistant* (1851), Oliver P. Smith's *The Domestic Architect* (1852 and 1854), and Charles P. Dwyer's *The Economic Cottage Builder* (1855 and 1856) and *The Economy of Church, Parsonage and School House Architecture Adapted to Small Societies and Rural Districts* (1856).

Like Dwyer's books, Smith's *Domestic Architect* must have been influential in southern Ontario, western New York State and Pennsylvania, and the Old Northwest Territory. At least one copy, however, went east: The American Life Foundation's copy was purchased in eastern Massachusetts where it had descended through several generations of Salem carpenters into the twentieth century!

An inquiry in 1974 to Professor Daniel D. Reiff, of the Art Department at State University College in Fredonia, New York, yielded the following information which he acknowledges as coming from Fredonia architect and teacher David G. Smith: "Oliver P. Smith practiced in the Ashville and Panama region, and is probably the architect of many of the fine Greek Revival houses in that area which are not documented. In Jewel Conover's *Nineteenth Century Architecture in Western New York* (1966) one house, p. 142 is given to O. Smith, and possibly the house on p. 131."

Hopefully, the republication of this rare book will help identify some of the historic buildings in the areas in which it was influential as well as illumine another corner of our Victorian architectural heritage.

THE

DOMESTIC ARCHITECT:

COMPRISING A SERIES OF

ORIGINAL DESIGNS

FOR

RURAL AND ORNAMENTAL COTTAGES,

WITH FULL AND COMPLETE EXPLANATIONS AND

DIRECTIONS TO THE BUILDER,

EMBRACING THE ELEMENTARY PRINCIPLES OF THE

Grecian and Cottage Styles,

WITH

PRIMARY RULES FOR DRAWING AND SHADING, AND THE RUDIMENTS OF LINEAR PERSPECTIVE.

Illustrated by over Two Hundred Engravings.

BY OLIVER P. SMITH,
ARCHITECT.

PUBLISHED BY PHINNEY & CO., BUFFALO.
IVISON & PHINNEY, NEW YORK.
1854.

JEWETT, THOMAS & CO.,
Stereotypers and Printers,
BUFFALO, N. Y.

PREFACE.

Any successful effort to improve the style and taste of the Domestic Architecture of our country cannot be otherwise than favorably regarded by the American public. It is a truth, acknowledged and deeply regretted by the most intelligent of our citizens, that the prevailing style of country building, in the United States, is exceedingly faulty. A great proportion of our houses — not excepting those of ambitious character and erected at large expense — are but incongruous piles, rude and cheerless in external appearance, and ill-contrived and comfortless within. And it is somewhat remarkable that this evil (it certainly *is* an evil) prevails most among farmers, and in country towns, where means are not wanting, and where room, raw material, and all the et ceteras for inside comfort and outside adornment are most abundant.

To correct this prevailing fault in the style of our Domestic Architecture — to introduce neat and tasteful dwellings in place of the deformed and repulsive tenements now scattered so thickly through the country — to adorn every village and town with beautiful residences and elegant villas — is a desideratum of high importance to the American people, and one which should elicit a large share of public attention. Nothing has more to do with the morals, the civilization, and refinement of a nation, than its prevailing Architecture. Virtue and Beauty are twin sisters; while Vice and Deformity are in constant association. The moral and refined seek a home where the virtuous influences that are ever reflected from Beauty and Order, are congenial to their cultivated minds and moral constitutions; while the coarse and vicious are best content with rude haunts, as barren of beauty as their own hearts of virtue. To the intelligent observer this fact is almost constantly visible, and is the subject of frequent remark. Indeed, it is instinctively understood by all. The traveler, in his journeyings, looks at the coarse dwelling, standing in repulsive naked-ness by the roadside, barren of all ornament, destitute of architectural symmetry and beauty, and with none of the surrounding adornments that encircle the home of quiet virtue, and secretly and instinctively the impression steals upon him, that the inmates of that dwelling are as coarse in mind and morals as the rude tenement they inhabit. Yet, when a little farther along, his eyes are greeted with a beautiful residence, tasteful in design, and symmetrical in all its parts, reposing within the shade of green maples and stately elms, and ornamented with wreaths of clambering vines, with a becoming grace and harmony in all its adornments and an air of cheerfulness and comfort pervading the entire scene, a silent yet impressive whisper tells him that Virtue and Happiness have there a congenial home — that Love and Social Refinement have there a sanctuary where the bitter fruits of vice and immorality are never tasted. The truthfulness of this picture will be readily acknowledged by the observing reader. And thus it is, the world over. Our minds and morals are subject to constant influence and modification, gradual yet lasting, by the inanimate walls with which we are surrounded. It has been well remarked, that every child is influenced for good or evil by the external objects with which it first grows familiar; and that nothing, except it be the teachings of a Christian mother, can do more toward moulding its character into virtuous shape, than Beauty, Order, and Symmetry, in its early home. How important, then, that the builders of our country should be thoroughly instructed in the business of their professions, since upon their judgment, skill, good taste, and knowledge of architecture, are we dependent for beauty, grace, and convenience of that dearest spot on earth, the centre and sanctuary of our social sympathies — HOME.

But, why is it that American builders — that is, beyond the limits of our most populous towns — are so imperfectly qualified for their business? Why is so large a proportion of our houses in the country and country towns constructed in total violation of architectural rules, and with little or no regard to taste, beauty, or convenience? Why is the Domestic Architecture prevailing in this country, so very coarse and ugly as to be a subject of remark, not only from intelligent Americans, but by foreigners? There is but one direct reply to these interrogations — *Our country builders are unprovided with a work on the science of Architecture suited to their wants.* There are, it is true, numerous works before the public that evince much talent and scientific knowledge on the part of the authors, and are, indeed, suited to the wants of a certain class of architects; but to the country builder, who stands in most need of elementary teaching, who wants the plainest and easiest rules in the rudiments of the science, they are in no wise adapted. And it is to supply this wide deficiency that I have prepared and now offer to the public, " THE DOMESTIC ARCHIETCT."

In this work I have not treated largely on the antique Grecian style of building, because I deemed it not as well suited to domestic purposes as the more modern styles of Cottage Architecture. Yet, for the benefit of those whose tastes may lead them to employ it, I have given a few, and, perhaps, a sufficient number of designs, for Entablatures, Columns, and Antes, to answer all practical purposes for the builder. The designs thus given are in the Grecian style, but not of Grecian example, yet such as may be used in structures of ordinary character, though not in those of the highest order of ornate finish.

Nor, in this treatise, have I entered upon the construction and adornment of the most costly and sumptuous dwellings; but have contented myself with furnishing the young student and country builder with a practical work on building, in which the elementary principles of the science are so simplified as to be easily and readily comprehended by the ordinary mechanic.

The primary rules for architectural drawing and shading, in elevation, section and detail, are given, together with the first principles of linear perspective. These instructions are given in language which, I trust, will be readily understood by the student. I have also furnished, in this work, a series of original designs of moderate cost, ranging from $500 to $7,000 each. In short, I have only studied to make the work *practical* and *useful* — one that shall instruct and assist the practical builder in the important business of his profession, and, through him, to aid in elevating the standard of Rural Architecture in this country from its present degraded position to a point of excellence more worthy of the American people. How far my humble endeavors shall prove successful, I wait patiently for the proof.

THE AUTHOR.

BUFFALO, September, 1852.

TO THE READER.

In most works on the subject of building, the authors have evidently presumed their readers well versed in the science of Geometry, and possessed of a thorough knowledge of geometrical terms, forgetting that the great majority of our country builders have had but limited means of acquiring a scientific education, and do not wish to craze their brains with words and terms not of ordinary use. When a figure is presented to them for practice, dictated by the rigid laws of geometrical precision, and explained in learned and classic phrase, they become bewildered and lost in a labyrinth of mysterious words and windings, and finally close the book disappointed and discouraged. I have therefore studiously avoided such perplexities to the unlearned student, and endeavored to simplify my explanations and present my figures with unmistakable directions for study and practice, using language and employing terms that cannot be misunderstood.

The classical reader will pardon this studied plainness, when he is informed that the great aim of this work is to furnish the mass of builders in the country and country villages with an easy system of Architecture, through which they may acquire a thorough knowledge of their business, both theoretically and practically, even to those of but ordinary literary attainments.

INDEX.

INTRODUCTORY REMARKS TO THE STUDENT.

The attention of the young student is earnestly invited to the subjoined rules and·directions:

1st. The student should make himself thoroughly acquainted with the lines and definitions illustrated on plate I, and explained on page 50. All this can be accomplished in a few hours, and the student will then find himself much better qualified to understand an architectural figure drawn for practical use than without such information.

2d. When the student wishes to trace the lines of an intricate figure, he should be careful to trace the notes of explanation, following the directions from reference to reference and from letter to letter, never advancing a single point in the figure until each preceding step is thoroughly understood. As, for instance, the author says in his notes: "Draw the line A B, as seen in the figure." Do so, and proceed no further until you look for the next directions; and thus continue to keep close and constant company with the author, until the figure is completed and thoroughly understood.

3d. When a figure or illustration is represented with a scale of feet and inches, take a pair of dividers and apply them to any part of the figure you wish to measure, and thus find the distance by the extended points of the dividers, and then apply them thus extended to the scale, and you will have the real distance, in feet and inches, of the part of the figure thus measured. And in like manner may you take an accurate measurement of each of the details of the figure.

4th. When you take up a design for a house, carefully examine its plan and elevation. Study its accommodations throughout, not hurriedly, but with care and deliberation. Read attentively the author's description and explanations. Should you find any apartment, the dimensions of which are not given, you can take an accurate measurement of the same, according to the directions given in the preceding rule. Should you find the plan of the house suited to your purpose, and yet are not satisfied with the decorations and finish, you may adopt the plan, and select such other finish as may better suit your taste, from illustrations given in detail, which are readily understood and easily measured for practical drawing.

5th. The student should turn to page 33, and study thoroughly the definitions there given; also, study well the glossary of technical terms.

6th. Acquaint yourself, by careful study, with the "General Rules to be observed by the Builder in practice," as given in another part of this work.

ANCIENT AND MODERN ARCHITECTURE.

There is not a subject of deeper or more thrilling interest in the whole wide field of history, than that of the origin, the progress, the vicissitudes and mutations of the science of building. Those nations which flourished long before the use of written characters was known, have left little or no other record of their glory and greatness than the relics of architectural piles, that for many tedious ages have defied the ravages of time, and now stand silent and sombre in the midst of barbarism and desolation, unfading monuments of the power and genius of those who fashioned them from the rude and shapeless rock. Little, indeed, *could* now be known of the power, the refinement and splendor of many nations that had their origin in remote ages of the world, but for these hoary relics of antiquity. No reliable written history concerning them is in existence. Their languages are blotted out; their names scarcely remembered; their national origin unknown; the very dates of their being buried deep in the tomb of oblivion; yet, the sculptured column, the curiously wrought cornice, the polished obelisk, the colossal statue, the vast temple, and the mighty pyramid, furnish indubitable proof that refinement in art, that high attainments in science, and that power, pomp, and splendor, existed among nations that had dwindled into contempt, or faded away, long anterior to the origin of ancient Greece.

But it was not our purpose to write a dissertation on the architectural relics of antiquity. We merely propose, in this place, to give a brief sketch of the several distinct styles of building now known, as it is a subject of peculiar interest to the architectural student. Noticing these styles in the order of their origin we first introduce the subject of

EGYPTIAN ARCHITECTURE.

Of the style of building practiced by the early settlers of Egypt, immediately after the Flood, the world is, and doubtless will ever remain, in the most profound ignorance. We can only *presume*, that the habitations of the primitive Egyptians were but very rude tenements, and that architecture was of slow and gradual growth through many centuries, assuming character, and advancing in the scale of arts and sciences, until the reign of Busiris, under whose supervision was built the renowned city of Thebes. It is enough to know, that architecture, as a science or as an art, can not be traced farther back than to the Egyptians, and that we know nothing of the state of perfection which it attained among that ancient people, except as we are taught by its vast remains, at this day the wonder and admiration of the world.

The Egyptian architecture is not so remarkable for its beauty of proportions, its harmony of parts, or its delicacy in ornament, as for the boldness of its design, the vastness of its structures, and its capacity for strength and endurance. It is capable of outliving all other works of art. Some of its vast piles have stood erect and almost unscathed, amid the ravages of war, and the waste and wane of time, while empires have risen, had their day, and expired —while nation succeeding nation has sprung out of the chaos of population, lived out its allotted centuries, and sunken into its oblivious sepulchre—proud, sombre, and silent, eternizing the power, the pomp, and glory of their forgotten builders.

The most renowned of the ancient cities of Egypt, and, without doubt, the most astonishing work of man that the world ever saw, was Thebes, the city of the hundred gates. "In the time of its splendor," says a modern writer, "it extended above twenty-three miles, and, upon an emergency, could send into the field, according to Tacitus, seven hundred thousand men.

"Though its walls were twenty-four feet in thickness, and its buildings the most solid and magnificent, yet, even in the time of Strabo and of Juvenal, only mutilated columns, broken obelisks, and temples leveled with the dust, remained to mark its situation, and inform the traveler of the desolating power which time, or the still more destructive hand of tyranny, can exert over the proudest monuments of human art."

"Thebes," says Strabo, "presents only remains of its former grandeur, dispersed over a space of eighty stadia in length. Here are found a great number of temples, in part destroyed by Cambyses; its inhabitants have retired to small towns east of the Nile, where the present city is built, and to the western shore, near Memnonium."

But we can not give the reader a better idea of architectural remains on the Nile, than by quoting from Mr. Stephen's description of the temples of Luxor and Carnac.

"On the Arabian side of the Nile are the great temples of Luxor and Carnac. The temple of Luxor stands near the bank of the river, built there, as is supposed, for the convenience of the Egyptian boatmen. Before the magnificent gateway of this temple, until within a few years, stood two lofty obelisks, each of a single block of red granite, more than eighty feet high, covered with sculpture and hieroglyphics, fresh as if but yesterday from the hands of the sculptor. One of them has been lately taken down by the French, and at this moment rears its daring summit to the skies in the center of admiring Paris; the other is yet standing on the spot where it was first erected.

"Between these and the grand propylon are two colossal statues with mitred headdresses; also, single blocks of marble, buried to the chest by sand, but still rising more than twenty feet above the ground. The grand propylon is a magnificent gateway, more than two hundred feet in length at its present base, and more than sixty feet above the sand. The whole front is covered with sculpture; the battle-scenes of an Egyptian warrior, designed and executed with extraordinary force and spirit. In one compartment, the hero is represented advancing at the head of his forces, and breaking through the ranks of his enemy; then standing, a colossal figure, in a car drawn by two fiery horses, with feathers waving over their heads, the reins tied round his body, his bow bent, the arrow drawn to its head, and the dead and wounded lying under the wheels of his car and the hoofs of his horses. In another place, several cars are seen at full speed for the walls of a town, fugitives passing a river, horses, chariots, and men, struggling to reach the opposite banks, while the hero, hurried impetuously beyond the rank of his own followers, is standing alone among the slain and wounded who have fallen under his formidable arm. At the farthest extremity, he is sitting on a throne as a conqueror, with a sceptre in his hand, a row of the principal captives before him, each with a rope around his neck; one, with outstretched hands, imploring pity, and another on his knees, to receive the blow of the executioner; while above is the vanquished monarch, with his hands tied to a car, about to grace the triumph of the conqueror.

"Passing this magnificent entrance, the visitor enters the dromas, or large open court, surrounded by a ruined portico, formed by a double row of columns covered with sculpture and hieroglyphics; and, working his way over heaps of rubbish and Arab huts, among stately columns, twelve feet in diameter, and between thirty and forty feet in height, some broken, with spreading capitals resembling the budding lotus, some prostrate, some half buried, and some lofty and towering as when they were first erected, at the distance of six hundred feet, reaches the sanctuary of the temple.

"But great and magnificent as was the temple of Luxor, it served but as a portal to the greater Carnac. Standing nearly two miles from Luxor, the whole road to it was lined with sphinxes, each of a single block of granite. At this end they are broken, and for the most part buried in the sand and heaps of rubbish. But approaching Carnac, they stand entire, still and solemn as when the ancient Egyptians passed between them to worship in the great temple of Ammon. Four great propylons terminate this avenue of sphinxes, and, passing through the last, the scene which presents itself surpasses description. Belzoni remarks of the ruins of Thebes, generally, that he felt as if he was in a city of giants; and no man can look upon the ruins of Carnac without feeling humbled by the greatness of a people who have passed away forever. The western entrance, facing the temple of Northern Dair, on the opposite side of the river, also approached between two rows of sphinxes, is a magnificent propylon, four hundred feet long and forty feet in thickness. In the language of Dr. Richardson, 'looking forward from the center of this gateway, the vast scene of havoc and destruction presents itself in all the extent of this immense temple, with its columns, and walls, and immense propylons, all prostrate in one heap of ruins, looking as if the thunders of heaven had smitten it at the command of an insulted God.'

"The field of ruins is about a mile in diameter; the temple itself, twelve hundred feet long, and four hundred and twenty broad. It has twelve principal entrances, each of which is approached through rows of sphinxes, as across the plain of Luxor, and each is composed of propylons, gateways, and other buildings, in themselves larger than most other temples; the sides of some of them are equal to the bases of most of the pyramids, and on each side of many are colossal statues, some sitting, others erect, from twenty to thirty feet in height. In front of the body of the temple is a large court, with an immense colonade on each side, of thirty columns in length, and through the middle two rows of columns fifty feet in height; then an immense portico, the roof supported by one hundred and thirty-four columns, from twenty-six to thirty-four feet in circumference. Next were four beautiful obelisks more than seventy feet high, three of which are still standing; and then the sanctuary, consisting of an apartment twenty feet square, the walls and ceiling of large blocks of highly polished granite, the ceiling studded with stars on a blue ground, and the walls covered with sculpture and hieroglyphics, representing offerings to Osiris, illustrating the mysterious uses of this sacred chamber, and showing the degraded character of the Egyptian worship. Beyond this is another colonade, and again porticoes and walls to another propylon, at a distance of two thousand feet from the western extremity of the temple."

But, notwithstanding the might, the vastness, and the grandeur which characterize the ancient architecture of Egypt, and though its sublime ruins afford a most exciting theme for the poet, and are justly the wonder and admiration of the modern world, yet the thought of exhuming it from the tomb of antiquity, and introducing it as a style of building in this, the noontide of civilization, and in a country where art and science are among the cherished idols of the people, is most revolting to the artist, and shocking to all who have a just appreciation of the age in which they live. It bears the marks of the superstitious age and the idolatrous nation in which it had its birth; and it were better that it remain undisturbed where it has slept in silence for ages past. There is a melancholy pleasure, as well as lessons of solemn instruction, in traversing its wide fields of desolation and marking the ceaseless waste of time upon its falling shafts and crumbling walls; but to introduce Egyptian architecture into modern use, would seem like robbing the sepulchre of its dead, and peopling the world with the skeletons of other times. The artist could never succeed in breathing into it the spirit of life; he might place it upright in the midst of modern art, but it would stand like a spectre from the tomb, mocking at those who had dragged it from the desolation of its native Nile.

Were I to select a situation in which to employ the ancient Egyptian style of building, with any regard to adaptation, and where it would have an expression of purpose, it would be in the construction of a felon's prison. Its massive and sepulchral appearance would impress upon the mind of the convict, as he approached its ponderous gates, the fixedness of his unhappy doom.

These general remarks on the subject of Egyptian architecture may seem insufficient to the reader; but I have deemed it unnecessary, to subserve the purposes of this work, to enter into a minute and detailed description of that ancient and now almost obsolete style of building.   Yet, to present to the mind of the student the leading characteristics of the architecture which prevailed on the shores of the Nile more than three thousand years since, I have furnished, on Plate XLII, three designs of Egyptian columns, with the peculiar ornaments of the Egyptian style.   On the column rests an entablature consisting of one huge concave moulding, in joinery, known as a cove or cavetto.   In the center of this entablature is a winged globe curiously ornamented, its wings sculptured into the concave surface of the entablature.

GRECIAN ARCHITECTURE.

As it is well known that the ancient Greeks were largely indebted to the Egyptians for early lessons in the arts and sciences, it may be presumed that they obtained their rudimentary notions of architecture from Egyptian artists.   Indeed, such a supposition may be very reasonably based upon the general resemblance of the two styles, though in detail and ornament they are widely different.   The Grecian, like the Egyptian style of architecture, consists of a column and entablature, and has many of the general characteristics of the latter; but it is carried to a state of perfection in proportion and adornment which the Egyptians had never reached.   The remains of Grecian architecture do not present such vast structures, colossal statues, towering obelisks, and immense labyrinthine tombs, as fill the mind of the traveler with awe and admiration on the banks of the Nile; yet they exhibit a style of building so perfect in proportions, so beautiful in design, and so chaste in ornament, as to be adopted as a model, with but slight improvements, through all subsequent ages.

The Grecian style or school of Architecture consists of three distinct Orders, which had their origin at different periods in the history of Greece. They are known as the Doric, Ionic, and Corinthian. The Grecians established a school of Architecture, by making the proportions and decorations of these three Orders different in every essential particular. And so well did they succeed, that every subsequent attempt to originate a new Order, has driven the artist to the necessity of borrowing, both in proportion and ornament, from some or all of these established Orders. The Romans attempted to add to the Grecian school, by introducing two new Orders with different proportions and decorations. The first of these was the Tuscan, which is but little unlike the Grecian Doric in proportions, yet is almost barren of its ornament, giving it a naked and uncouth appearance absolutely repulsive to the eye. It is very seldom employed at the present day, and many modern writers pronounce it entirely unfit for use. The next was the Composite, which has nearly the proportions of the Corinthian, with decorations taken from both Corinthian and Ionic. The capital is the distinguishing characteristic of an Order; yet this Order has the leaves of the Corinthian capital, combined with the volutes of the Ionic. Hence its name, the *Composite*. It is very seldom employed in this country, for it seems to be generally conceded that the Grecian school of Architecture is complete without—its orders rising from the plain and massive Doric to the light and rich proportions of the Corinthian.

The Doric Order is the first, and the plainest and heaviest of the three Grecian Orders. Its column has a plain moulded capital, broad, flat flutes, and is without a base. Its entablature is decorated with plain angular triglyphs, said to resemble ends of beams, and mutules on the soffit of the corona resembling the ends of rafters. It is not expensive, and is much used in this country. When judiciously employed in structures of great magnitude, it has a grand and pleasing appearance. Modern builders often use it in unimportant structures, leaving off the triglyphs and mutules, and sometimes changing the profile of the cornice, but in the column making little or no modification. This departure from Doric principles may be tolerated in many places where columns are necessary, as it tends very much to lessen expense, and yet answers our purpose.

The Grecians next founded the Ionic Order, designing it to have a lighter and more airy appearance than the Doric. Its column has a greater number of diameters in height; its capital consists of four scrolls, or volutes, at each angle of the abacus, with an enriched echinus and astragal encircling the top of the column. The column has a greater number of flutes in its shaft than the Doric, though it is much smaller; the shaft stands upon a base consisting of a combination of plain mouldings. The cornice consists of a combination of mouldings sometimes enriched with sculpture, and with dentils or blocks placed at regular intervals in the bed moulding. It is not as expensive as the Doric, and it is employed, to a considerable extent, in the United States, but not as frequently as the Doric in structures of moderate size, owing, without doubt, to its being more difficult to execute the capital. The entablature is much cheaper than in either of the other Orders, and is therefore frequently used without the column, as the Doric column is sometimes used without the Doric entablature, substituting one of less expense.

When the Ionic is well employed, it gives a beautiful and

pleasing appearance, and occupies the middle ground between the plain, republican Doric and the rich and sumptuous Corinthian.

The last and most ornate of the Grecian Orders, is the Corinthian. It was founded at a period when pomp, splendor, and voluptuous prodigality reigned in many of the Grecian states. It is still lighter than the Ionic, and highly enriched with sculpture. Its capital is shaped like an inverted bell, encircled with two rows of Acanthus leaves. In the capital are eight small volutes or scrolls placed at intervals under the abacus. The column has a greater number of diameters in height than the Ionic, yet with the same number of flutes in the shaft. It stands upon a base consisting of a combination of mouldings richer and more complicated than the Ionic base. Its entablature is highly enriched with sculptured mouldings. The soffit of the corona is ornamented with sculptured modillions, placed at regular intervals.

The Corinthian Order is said to have had its origin in the following circumstance: A young Corinthian female, possessed of rare personal charms and accomplishments, died, just as she had arrived at the age considered by the Corinthians as marriageable. Her nurse, who dearly loved her, placed a basket of trinkets over her grave, and happening to leave it on a bed of Acanthus roots, in due time the stalk and leaves grew up around it; and, there being a flat stone or tile on the top to keep out the storm, some of the stalks reached the surface projecting from the basket, and twined over, somewhat resembling volutes. Calamachus, an eminent Grecian sculptor, happening to pass the basket at this time, the appearance suggested to his mind the idea of a new Order in Architecture. Its name is derived from its Corinthian origin.

The Corinthian Order is rich and beautiful in appearance, and occupies the highest place in the Grecian school of Architecture. It is not as much employed in this country as either of the other Grecian Orders, and for two reasons: first, it is too gay; and second, of too great expense.

GOTHIC ARCHITECTURE.

The Gothic style of Architecture had its origin in the middle ages, when the arts were just beginning to revive after the siege and plundering of Rome by the Goths. The name *Gothic* would lead one to suppose that this style owed its origin to the rude and barbarous people who were the enemies and destroyers, rather than the friends and promoters of the arts, in Southern Europe. That people, however, had nothing to do with its origin or introduction to European practice. Its name was given to it by English architects, as a stigma, on account of its wide departure from the Antique or Grecian style. It was introduced into England, France, Germany, and other parts of Europe, six or eight centuries ago. Its principles differ, in almost every particular, from Grecian. It might have had its origin in imitation of clustered groves and bowers, under which the Druids of that day assembled to worship and perform their religious rites. Its chief distinguishing features are, the general predominance of the perpendicular over the horizontal; its clustered pillars and vaulted roofs; its pinnacles, pointed arches, and lofty spires; its massive buttresses, and its great and almost endless profusion of decoration.

Although the Gothic style had its origin at a very dark period of time, yet it is possessed of many and great excellencies, and has given rise to some of the most extensive, grand, and imposing structures of modern times.

From the perfect dissimilarity of character and features, between the Grecian and Gothic styles of Architecture, it may with propriety be said, that they constitute the only two distinct and independent styles now in existence. All other styles partake of some of the characteristics of one or the other of these; yet they have not a single feature in common; the one has not a single mark or proportion borrowed from the other. And it is hardly possible to erect a structure of any considerable magnitude, without its being marked with some of the characteristics of one or both of these styles. Hence, they stand as proud monuments of artistic genius, invincible against the combined skill and ingenuity of modern artists.

COTTAGE ARCHITECTURE.

Out of the Gothic has arisen a modern style of domestic Architecture, bringing with it some of the characteristics of its great original, yet without the cumbrous complications which mark the Gothic when used for ecclesiastical purposes. It was first employed in the reign of Henry VII, and within the last century has become very prevalent in England, particularly in the vicinity and suburbs of London.

The Cottage style is well suited to domestic purposes, and harmonizes admirably with the picturesque rural scenery of this country. It is no more expensive than the Grecian style, in the degenerate form in which that is now employed, yet is more convenient and far more beautiful. One of the great advantages of this style of building is this, that a residence may be erected to suit the means of the proprietor, from the plain and unostentatious farm-house to the highly-enriched and elegant country villa. But as this work is principally devoted to Cottage Architecture, further remark of this style need not here be made. Its peculiar beauties and advantages over other styles of building, may best be understood by studying it in detail.

It might be proper to remark, before closing this article, that there are many different forms or fashions of building prevailing in various countries, that have no strict conformity to the styles herein noticed, yet none possessing sufficient merit to take rank in the schools of architectural science. The Chinese, the Turks, and people of other distinct political divisions of the earth, have each their fashions of building; yet they are possessed of little in the line of Architecture worthy of imitation in a country of common civilization.

GENERAL RULES TO BE OBSERVED BY THE BUILDER IN PRACTICE.

The experienced and skillful builder will readily perceive that many of the following rules are more particularly directed to beginners and those of little experience.

FOUNDATIONS.

In the foundations for architectural structures—and particularly those of brick or stone—care should be taken that the walls be laid on solid earth, hard-pan, or rock.

In building dwarf-walls, or underpinning, it is necessary to place the foundation stone nearly or quite two feet below the surface, even should solid earth or hard-pan be found at a less depth,—it is important to prevent the action of frost.

In every cellar or foundation wall, an aperture or opening should be left for the escape of impure air.

The foundation walls to a framed building should be one inch larger than the sills, on every side of the building. This is necessary to bring the walls flush with the finish above.

Water-tables in stone or brick buildings should project from one and a half to two inches.

SIDING.

When the siding or covering of a frame is placed in a horizontal position, the boards should be lapped in the manner of common siding. Such boards, rabbetted and dressed to a thickness on the upper edge, make a very substantial covering; matched boards by tongue and groove are not as durable, the joints being exposed to early decay by the admission and retention of moisture. Feather edge is preferable to matching. But boards placed in a *perpendicular* position are the most durable.

INTERCOLUMNIATION.

Intercolumniation is the distance between columns. It is difficult to determine the distance which columns should be placed apart, in the front of an edifice, as the width of the front and number of openings control, to a great extent, their position—for columns should never stand before the openings of windows or doors. Hence, a wide and low front, with few openings, would give the range of columns an exceedingly bad appearance, in consequence of their great distance apart, in proportion to their size and height, and the apparent weight they are presumed to sustain.

The following directions may answer, in most cases, a tolerable purpose, in arranging a colonade front:

Let the height and width of the building conform to the number of openings, in such a manner as, that the distance between two columns added to the diameter of one of the columns, will not exceed half of the height of the column. For instance, we propose to construct a front twenty-four feet wide with three openings. To find a proper height for the front: divide the twenty-four feet by three, (which is the number of spaces,) and the quotient will be eight feet; multiply eight by two, which gives the height of the columns, sixteen feet. To this add the height of the entablature, which is two diameters of a column, and you will then have the entire height of the front. In very high buildings, the spaces may be less than one-half, and, often, as near as one-third of the height of the column.

The method here given is not presumed to be an infallible rule, nor is it designed as one to be strictly followed in every instance; yet the builder will find it a sort of basis upon which to found his design and arrangement for the front of a building. If he should perceive, when maturing a design for a house, that the columns will have a greater distance apart than will accord with the above rule, he should change his conceptions of the front, and, either change its breadth, add to the number of openings, or increase the height of the building.

This difficulty in design often occurs in porticoes, which occupy but a single story of a dwelling, and where the columns must necessarily have a greater distance apart than half their height, by reason of the openings in the front, and also to secure purposes of convenience in passing between them.

ANTES AND ENTABLATURES.

Antes or Pilasters should never be placed under an entablature, unless the entablature has nearly or quite its proper height, according to the regular rules for proportioning an order. The same rule applies to columns, though a deformity of this character is not as often practiced when columns are employed as with the antes.

WINDOW AND DOOR OPENINGS.

The arrangement of window and door openings in the fronts of buildings, where neither columns nor antes are employed, is a subject which merits at least a passing remark. To regulate and arrange the piers and openings in the front of such buildings, the builder will find the following method as generally applicable:

Suppose the front of a house to be thirty feet in width and twenty feet high, in which we propose to have four openings, requiring, necessarily, five piers. Ascertain from the height of the front, the proper breadth of an ante to occupy such a place. Mark off the space of that breadth from each corner of the front inward. Then divide the intermediate space into equal divisions, and determine the locations of the three other antes, thus designating the places for five antes, standing equidistant from each other in the thirty feet front. Then locate your windows precisely in the centre of the intervals between the *supposed* antes. So that windows in a building *without* antes, should be placed precisely as they would be in a building *with* antes. It should be observed that this rule is particularly designed for the principal front rather than flanks of a building.

Openings should be placed over openings, and piers over piers. This rule should be as rigidly observed where there are no columns or antes to regulate the disposition of windows, as with them.

The height of windows should be made to conform to the height of the rooms in which they are placed. Small, low windows in a high room, will disfigure both the inside and outside appearance of the building. Again, broad windows, not divided into two or more compartments, are in bad taste, and should be avoided.

Windows should not be placed too far below the ceiling; neither should they be too near to admit of a suitable and corresponding style of finish with the other portions of the same room.

It is highly important, in the external finish of windows, to have a wise regard to their decoration; for windows are certainly an important feature and portion of a dwelling.

FLOOR AND CEILING TIMBERS.

Never frame joists into beams or girders that extend across the centre or any part of the ceiling of a room, as the walls are very apt to crack on the line where the joists come in contact with the beam. It is better that a single joist extend over the entire width of a room, (or length, as the case may be,) in order that the downward pressure may be equally distributed, and not fall on any single point. Even in rooms of twenty-five feet span, the joists should reach from wall to wall.

VENTILATION.

It is a matter of the utmost importance that every room in a house be well ventilated. The escape of impure air should be in the ceiling, or near the top of a room. There should also be an opening at the bottom of a room for the admission of pure air from the open atmosphere. This should be on the opposite side of the room from the ventilator, the better to give a uniform circulation of air throughout the room. The apparatus for ventilating every room in a house is a matter of but trifling expense, as the impure air can be very easily conducted to the chimney flues by means of a ventiduct.

As the subject of ventilation is one of more than ordinary importance, and one with which the builder should become thoroughly acquainted, I have treated of it more at length in another article of this work, under the head of "Heat and Ventilation." To that article the reader's attention is respectfully invited.

REMARKS ON DESIGNING.

In designing a dwelling, the qualifications of the first importance with the builder, are *taste* and *judgment*. It is his business to study the best interests of his employer, and, in maturing a design, to consult *economy* as earnestly as if he were planning for himself.

The builder should take into consideration: 1st, The ground to be occupied; 2d, The amount of room requisite for the convenience of the family; and, 3d, The amount of money to be employed in the construction of the house. These are three important considerations which should ever be kept in view, and each accommodated to the others according to the dictates of good sense. The builder should arrange the several apartments of the house with a studied regard for convenience, but *not* at the sacrifice of symmetry and order in the outside contour of the building. It is the poorest economy to destroy the external beauty of a dwelling by throwing it into repulsive disproportion for some unimportant considerations of convenience within. These clashing considerations which frequently involve the builder in serious perplexity are, however, very easily obviated in the modern style of cottage architecture, giving to this new style a decided preference over the square form of the antique Grecian, especially when used for domestic purposes.

The broken and irregular form of the modern cottage style, with its pointed gables, projecting wings, and bay windows, gives it the advantage of admitting light into every apartment, without destroying the symmetry of contour. And another advantage which adds much value to the modern style, is, that we may construct only a part of a house, and at a subsequent time add other apartments to the original structure without giving them the appearance of awkward and disjointed additions. It is important, however, that the plan of any such additions be anticipated and fully matured in the original design. Then the portions that are afterwards added, may combine symmetrically with the original structure, and all appear as if united at the same time.

The man who contemplates building a house of any considerable importance, in point of expense, can not be too strongly urged to employ an architect of talent and experience to furnish him a design, with plans and specifications in detail, of the entire structure. He will find the advantages vastly outweigh the expense. Certainly, if he desires a residence that is truly convenient, tasteful and elegant, and wishes to observe the strictest economy in the erection of his house, he will never trust to his own skill and judgment for a plan, unless he is himself an architect of skill and experience. Let us see how it works: I have a friend who regards himself as a model economist; yet, he has a trifling litigation in which he pays a lawyer twenty or twenty-five dollars, because, he says, he is himself *no lawyer;* but, when he is about to erect a costly residence, in which he expects to spend the remainder of his life, he imagines he can "save something," by planning his own house, forgetting that it is not only true that he is "no lawyer," but that it is equally true that he is *no architect.* Now, what is the result of this very common mode of financiering? My friend, indeed, retains twenty-five dollars which he should have paid to a competent architect. But he soon finds much to perplex him in directing his mechanics. Much of their time is wasted in learning *his* peculiar arrangement. His building material is not of the proper quality, nor apportioned in the proper quantities. But, worst of all, he finds, when his house is finished, that it has cost him the snug little sum of $2,500, and yet is not suited to his wants. The inside arrangement is awkward ·and ill-contrived. The outside is disproportioned, clumsy, and repulsive. He is dissatisfied with the whole affair. He would give *five hundred dollars* to change the plan, to re-model it according to his now *enlightened* notions of architecture. He finds, in fact, when too late, that the $25 "saved" by refusing to employ an architect, in whose skill and judgment he could confide, has proved a *loss*, with more than ten-fold the amount added. And this is the true and certain result of such a policy. It is much more possible for a man to convert himself into a well-read and skillful lawyer with a single day's study, than to make a competent architect of himself in a like period.

The above remarks may seem like a digression, yet I wish them to serve an object directly in point. The evil mentioned above may be remedied. The builder should understand better the business of his profession. He should not content himself with being a mere mechanic, but should qualify himself as an *architect*. He should acquaint himself with the art of drawing and designing. Too long has he been content to follow the plans of his employer.

Were the mechanics who do the principal part of the building among farmers and in country towns, properly qualified in the business of their professions, they would soon find their employers willing to resign the business of designing into the hands to which it legitimately belongs. A knowledge of designing and drawing is, indeed, of greater importance to the builder in the country than to those living in the city, because the latter have a much better opportunity to employ the services of a professional architect.

To assist the builder in planning dwellings, I have given, on Plate XXVI, a series of designs by outline sketches, in ground plan and elevation, sufficiently varied in point of cost and arrangement to meet the necessities of the less opulent, and to accommodate those whose means and tastes lead them to erect commodious and even elegant country residences. The decorations and finish of these designs are, however, left entirely to the taste and judgment of the builder; and he should be carefully discriminating in selecting the style of finish to be employed. One form of house will not admit of the same style of its adornments of some other. On a large, two-story house, with broad gables, brackets are the most suitable. On a high house, with hipped roof, consoles and stalactends should be employed. On a house with numerous high pointed gables, the fringe, or ornamental barge and pendant, is most suitable. The cornice is the leading characteristic of the cottage style, and it is, therefore, highly essential to continue a marked resemblance of form throughout the entire building. Yet a change in the features and detail of these decorations, as they appear in different positions on the same structure, is not only unobjectionable, but really desirable, since variety is always essential to picturesque beauty.

The builder should study the convenience and accommodations of the several designs on Plate XXVI, and should he find a plan nearly answering his purpose, a little deviation from its present arrangement might render it quite acceptable. Hence, by exercising a little taste and skill in the change, this single plate may be used as a platform, from which he may originate designs conforming to the tastes and wishes of nearly all who may require his services.

DEFINITION OF TERMS OFTEN OCCURRING IN PRACTICE.

Arris; an edge formed by the meeting of two curves in a moulding, as in the flutes of a Doric column.

Acanthus; an ornament resembling the foliage or leaves of the plant acanthus, used in the capitals of the Corinthian and Composite Orders.

Barge-board; a board which serves as a finish at the termination of a roof with the gable, and sometimes wrought into a kind of drapery, in which case it becomes a leading feature in decoration.

Bay-window; a window projecting from the wall, with several

compartments, and forming a kind of bay to the room to which it is attached.

BRACKET; a kind of brace placed at regular intervals under the projection of a roof in Cottage Architecture.

BISECT; to divide into two equal parts.

CHORD; a straight line from one point of an arch to the other, the base of an arch; the direct line from one termination of the segment of a circle to the other.

COLOSSAL; like a Colossus; very large; huge; gigantic.

COLOSSUS; a statue of gigantic size. The most remarkable Colossus of antiquity was one at Rhodes, a statue of Apollo, so high that, it is said, ships might sail between its legs.

CORRIDOR; a long passage leading to the several apartments in an edifice.

CONE; a solid figure, having a circle for its base and terminating with an apex, like the small end of a sugar-loaf.

CONSOLE; a kind of sculptured bracket, serving to support the cornice in Cottage Architecture.

DELINEATE; to draw the lines which exhibit the form of anything; to mark out with lines; to make a draught; to represent a picture; to draw a likeness.

DETAILS; figures representing the several departments of a structure.

DRAPERY; light and airy decorations, representing trees, plants, and festoons of cloth, in ornamental architecture.

DENTIL; rectangular blocks in the bed moulds of the Ionic and Corinthian Orders.

ELEVATION; the true representation of an object or building, drawn from mathematical principles by a scale.

FIGURE; a diagram; the form of anything, as expressed by the outline or terminating extremities. A *triangle* is a figure of three sides.

FRINGE; a sculptured ornament, decorating the cornice in Cottage Architecture.

MINARETS; a slender and lofty turret in Turkish Architecture.

MULLION; an upright bar and division in a window-frame.

NICHE; a cavity, hollow, or recess, within the thickness of a wall, for a statue, bust, or other erect ornament.

OCTAGON; a figure having eight sides.

ORTHOGRAPHY; the art of delineating or drawing the front of an object, and exhibiting the heights or elevations of the several parts; so called because it determines things by perpendicular lines falling on the geometrical plane.

PROTRACTOR; a mathematical instrument for laying down and measuring angles on paper, used in drawing or plotting. It is of various forms; semi-circular, rectangular, and circular.

PENDANT; a hanging ornament on roofs, ceilings, &c., much used in Gothic and Cottage Architecture.

PERSPECTIVE; the application of geometrical principles to drawing on a plain surface, true resemblances or pictures of objects, as the objects appear to the eye from any given distance or situation, real or imaginary.

PINNACLE; a slender turret or part of a building elevated above the main building; a high, spiring point; summit.

QUADRANT; the quarter of a circle, or the quarter of the circumference of a circle.

RADIUS; a right line drawn or extending from the centre of a circle to the periphery; the semi-diameter of the circle.

RADII; the plural of *radius*.

REGISTER; a lid, stopper, or sliding plate, in a furnace, stove, &c., for regulating the admission of air and the heat of the fire.

SEGMENT; a part cut off from a figure by a line or plane, as the segment of a sphere, the segment of a colyx—a part or segment of an arch.

SECTOR; a part of a circle comprehended between two radii and the including arch; or a mixed triangle formed by two radii and the arch of a circle; a mathematical instrument, so marked with lines of signs, tangents, secants, chords, &c., and used in finding the proportion between quantities of the same kind.

SECTION; the art of cutting or of separating by cutting; the representation of an object, as a building, machine, &c., cut asunder vertically, so as to show the interior or profile; a part separated from the rest; a division.

VENTIDUCT; a conductor of air.

VESTIBULE; the porch or entrance into a house, or large, open space before the door, but covered; a little antechamber before the entrance of an ordinary apartment.

VERTICAL; the opposite angles formed by two intersecting straight lines.

VERANDA; an Oriental word, denoting a kind of open portico, formed by extending a sloping or covered roof beyond the main building.

HEAT AND VENTILATION.

It is a fact now generally known, that life and health can not be maintained without a constant supply of pure air; and that every room, whether for public resort, where large numbers meet for religious worship, for business, or for pleasure, or in the private dormitory, where only a single family are breathing in the same small limit of atmosphere, is incomplete and unfit for the reception of human beings, until it is furnished with the means of a constant supply of fresh air immediately from the great fountain without.

We find this subject so ably treated of in Barnard's School Architecture, that we can not better serve our purpose than to copy from that work:

"The atmosphere which surrounds our earth to the height of forty-five miles, and in which we live, and move, and have our being, is composed mainly of two ingredients, oxygen and nitrogen, with a slight admixture of carbonic acid. The first is called the life principle, the breath of life, because by forming and purifying the blood it alone sustains life, and supports combustion. But to sustain these processes, there is a constant consumption of this ingredient going on, and, as will be seen by the facts in the case, the formation and accumulation of another ingredient, carbonic acid, which is deadly hostile to animal life and combustion. This gas is sometimes found in wells, and will then extinguish a lighted candle if lowered into it, (and which always should be lowered into a well before any person ventures down,) and is not an uncommon cause of death in such places. It is almost always present in deep mines, and at the bottom of caverns.   Near Naples there is one of this description, called the Grotto del Cane, or the Grotto of the Dog, because the guides who accompany strangers to the interesting spots in the vicinity of Naples, usually take a dog along with them to show the effects of this gas upon animal life. Being heavier than common air, it flows along the bottom of the cavern, and although it does not reach as high as the mouth or nostrils of a grown man, no sooner does a dog venture into it, than the animal is seized with convulsions, gasps, and would die if not dragged out of it into the pure air.   When recovered, the dog shows no more disposition to return to the cavern.   *   *   *   *

"This air which we breathe, if pure, when taken into the mouth and nostrils, is composed in every one hundred parts, of 21 oxygen, 78 nitrogen, and 1 of carbonic acid.   After traversing the innumerable cells into which the lungs are divided and subdivided, and then coming into close contact with the blood, these proportions are essentially changed, and when breathed out, the same quantity of air contains 8 per cent. less of oxygen and 8 per cent. more of carbonic acid.   If in this condition, (without being renewed,) it is breathed again, it is deprived of another quantity of oxygen, and loaded with the same quantity of carbonic acid.   Each successive act of breathing reduces in this way, and in this proportion, the vital principle of the air, and increases in the same proportion that which destroys life.   But, in the meantime, what has been going on in the lungs, with regard to the blood?   This fluid, after traversing the whole frame, from the heart to the extremities, parting all along with its heat, and ministering its nourishing particles to the growth and preservation of the body, returns to the heart changed in color, deprived somewhat of its vitality, and loaded with impurities.   In this condition, for the purpose of renewing its color, its vitality, and its purity, it makes the circuit of the lungs, when by means of innumerable vessels, inclosing, like a delicate network, each individual air cell, every one of its finest particles comes into close contact with the air which has been breathed. If this air has its due proportion of oxygen, the color of the blood changes from a dark purple to a bright scarlet; its vital warmth is restored, and its impurities, by the union of the oxygen of the air with the carbon of blood, of which these impurities are made up, are thrown off in the form of carbonic acid. Thus vitalized and purified, it enters the heart to to be again sent out through the system on its errand of life and beneficence, to build up and repair the solid frame-work of the body, give tone and vigor to its muscles, and restring all its nerves to vibrate in unison with the glorious sights and thrilling sounds of nature, and the still, sad music of humanity.

"But in case the air with which the blood comes in contact, through the thin membranes that constitute the cells of the lungs, does not contain its due proportion of oxygen, viz: 20 or 21 per cent., as when it has once been breathed, then the blood returns to the heart unendued with newness of life, and loaded with carbon and other impurities which unfit it for the purposes of nourishment, the repair and maintenance of the vigorous actions of all the parts, and especially of the brain and spinal column, the great fountains of nervous power. If this process is long continued, even though the air be but slightly deteriorated, the effects will be evident in the languid and feeble action of the muscles, the sunken eye, the squalid hue of the skin, the unnatural irritability of the nervous system, a disinclination to all mental and bodily exertion, and a tendency to stupor, headache, and fainting. If the air is very impure, i. e. has but little or no oxygen and much carbonic acid, then the imperfect and poisoned blood will act with a peculiar and malignant energy on the whole system, and especially on the brain, and convulsions, apoplexy, and death must ensue.

"* * * * The necessity of renewing the atmosphere does not arise solely from the consumption of the oxygen, and the constant generation of carbonic acid, but from the presence of other destructive agents and impurities. There is carburetted hydrogen, which Dr. Dunglinson, in his Physiology, characterizes, 'as very depressing to the vital functions. Even when largely diluted with atmospheric air, it occasions vertigo, sickness, diminution of the force and velocity of the pulse, reduction of muscular vigor and every symptom of diminished power.' There is also sulphuretted hydrogen, which the same author says, in its pure state, kills instantly, and in its diluted state, produces powerful sedative effects on the pulse, muscles, and whole nervous system. There are also destructive and offensive impurities arising from the decomposition of animal and vegetable matter in contact with the stove, or dissolved in the evaporating dish.

"The objects to be obtained [by ventilation] are, the removal of such impurities as have been referred to, and which are constantly generated, wherever there is animal life and burning fires, and the due supply of that vital principle, which is constantly consumed by breathing and combustion. The first can be in no other way effectually secured, but by making provision for its escape into the open air, both at the top and bottom of the room; and the second, but by introducing a current of pure air from the outside of the building, warmed in winter by a furnace, or in some other mode, before entering the room. The processes should go on together, i. e. the escape of the vitiated air from within, and the introduction of the pure air from without. The common fireplace and chimney secures the first object very effectually, for there is always a strong current of air near the floor, towards the fire, to support combustion, and supply the partial vacuum in the chimney occasioned by the ascending column of smoke and rarified air, and in this current the carbonic acid and other impurities will be drawn into the fire and up the chimney. But there is such an enormous waste of heat in these fireplaces, and such a constant influx of cold air through every crevice in the imperfect fittings of the doors and windows, to supply the current always ascending the chimney, that this mode of ventilation, should not be relied on. The common mode of ventilating by opening a window or door, although better than none, is also imperfect and objectionable, as the cold air falls directly on the head, neck, and other exposed parts of the body, when every pore is open, and thus causes discomfort, catarrh, and other more serious evils, to those sitting near, besides reducing the temperature of the whole room too suddenly and too low."

The only perfect system of supplying a room in winter with pure, warm air, is by means of a furnace situated in the cellar or under the building. The furnace should be constantly and abundantly supplied with fresh, out-door air, which should be heated only sufficiently to give each room to which it is conducted the desired temperature, as overheating destroys the vital properties of the air. It is better, too, that the register or aperture, through which the air from the furnace is admitted into a room, be sufficient to admit a large current of air, thus warming the room with air of a lower temperature than would be required were the current of air admitted through a smaller register. The register should be constructed with a slide to regulate the temperature of the room at pleasure. A house thus furnished with a furnace communicating with each of the several rooms, and with each of its rooms properly ventilated, excluding all atmospheric impurities, is made healthy and comfortable for its inmates, by having a constant supply of pure air and an even temperature.

It is not proposed, in this work, to give instructions as to the mode of constructing furnaces, as there are already abundant sources of such information. I have only endeavored to impress on the mind of the reader the importance of heating and ventilating every room where human beings are to congregate, with a wise reference to the laws of life and health.

GRECIAN ORDERS DEFINED.

In Grecian Architecture there are three Orders, denominated the Doric, the Ionic, and the Corinthian.

By an *Order* is meant, the proportion and decoration of an Entablature and Column. Each Order has a proportion and decoration differing from those of any other, and has, therefore, its own peculiar character and individuality.

An Order has two Divisions: the Entablature and the Column.

The Entablature has three Divisions: the Cornice, the Frieze, and the Architrave. The Column has also three Divisions, (excepting the Doric:) the Capital, the Shaft, and the Base. The Doric has no Base.

Each of these Divisions has a combination of members of different outline and proportion, yet each Order has members by position, though not by outline, that are common to all the Orders. The most important of these members, or details of a Division in an Order, are given and defined in the following catalogue:

CROWN MOULD; the upper member of the Cornice.

CORONA; the main projection of the Cornice.

BED MOULD; mouldings under the Corona.

ABACUS; the upper member of a Capital.

ECHINUS; the member next below the Abacus in the Doric Capital, and directly below the Flanks of the Volutes in the Ionic.

APOPHYGEE; the curve that forms the easing, joining the Capital and Shaft, or Shaft with the Base.

PROPORTIONS OF THE GRECIAN ORDERS.

THE DORIC ORDER.—To proportion and draw the Doric Order: Divide the entire height of the building—that is, the space which the Order is to occupy—into nine equal parts. Then take *one* of those nine parts—that is, *one-ninth* of the space from the top of the cornice to the bottom of the column—and you will have the proper diameter of the Doric Column at the bottom. You will then take the diameter of the column, thus obtained, and divide it into *sixty* equal parts, which are called *minutes*, and are to be used as a scale of proportion.

THE IONIC ORDER.—To proportion and draw the Ionic Order: Divide the space which the Order is to occupy into *ten* or *eleven* equal parts, and one of those parts will be the diameter of the column contiguous to the base. Divide the diameter of the column, thus obtained, into *sixty* equal parts, as in the Doric. You will then have a scale of minutes, from which the height and projection may be easily taken from a copy of the Ionic Order.

THE CORINTHIAN ORDER.—Proportions are made in the Corinthian Order as in the Doric and Ionic, except that the altitude to be occupied by the Order is first divided into *twelve* parts, to obtain the diameter of a column. One diameter is divided into sixty parts for a scale of minutes, as above directed.

SCALE OF MINUTES.

To make a scale by which to draw the Doric Order: Divide the height of the building (that is, the space from the top of the cornice to the bottom of the column,) into nine equal parts. Then *one* of the nine parts thus found is the proper diameter at the bottom.

Let us suppose a building, for which we wish to make a scale, is eighteen feet high. Dividing that height into nine equal parts, would give two feet as the diameter of the column at the bottom. We will cut a smooth piece of lath just two feet long, and with a pair of dividers mark it off into six equal divisions, drawing lines with a knife or pencil point across the lath, to designate the divisions. We will next divide *one* of these six divisions on the piece of lath into *ten* equal parts. We shall then have our scale complete, the *small* divisions being called *minutes*. By this process, it will be seen that one diameter of the column at the bottom measures *sixty minutes*—for the diameter is first divided into *six* parts, and one of these into *ten*, which is equivalent to dividing the whole diameter into sixty equal divisions.

Having thus found the method of obtaining the scale, we will next proceed to draw an entablature of full size, for practice, by the scale from the example on Plate V, Fig. 1. On a smooth board of sufficient length, draw a perpendicular line for the face of the frieze, and one at right angle from it for the top of the crown mould. The columns of figures at the left of Fig. 1 will designate the number of minutes in the *height* and *projection* of the several members in the Order. Thus, the figures standing below H, designate (in minutes,) the *height* of the members; and those below P, their *projection.*

Now, take from the scale of minutes, which you have just made, eight minutes, and set the distance below the line drawn for the top of the crown mould; and draw a line parallel with the top line, to designate the *bottom* of the crown mould. Then take from the scale fourteen minutes, as seen below H, for the height of the facia; then forty minutes for the frieze, and so on, till you have given the height of the several members to the bottom of the entablature. Then set off twenty-nine minutes from the frieze line as the projection of the crown mould; draw a perpendicular line across the width of the crown mould at the point of its projection; then twenty-six for the projection of the facia, and four for the architrave as seen in the column of figures under the letter P.

For the capital of the column, take the same scale, and proceed in a similar manner, making the projection from the face of the column.

RUDIMENTS OF ARCHITECTURAL DRAWING.

It is not proposed, in this article, to enter into a systematic treatise on the important art of architectural drawing, but merely to throw out a few hints and directions which may be of use to the beginner.

The student, before attempting the art of drawing, should provide himself with a case of mathematical instruments, a drawing board and a T. (The T is a kind of square somewhat resembling a trying-square, the shanks extending each way from the blade.) He should also provide himself with drawing-paper, a few sable pencil brushes—camel's hair brushes are not as good—some India ink, a few good water-color paints, and a fine soft lead pencil. The water colors should embrace Carmine, or Lake, Prussian Blue, Gamboge for yellow, Bister or Burnt Umber for brown, and Indian Red. For the different shades of green, mix blue with yellow.

To prepare the paper on the drawing-board, moisten both sides of it with a soft sponge before placing it upon the board. After the paper is spread upon the board, turn up the edges about one-fourth of an inch, and spread upon them a preparation of glue; then, with an ivory scale, press down the edges to the board, and rub frequently over them, to assist the glue in setting before the paper shrinks and becomes detached from the board. The paper is slightly moistened, in order to cause it to expand; then, when its edges are firmly attached to the board, it will gradually shrink by drying, and thus strain itself smoothly over the surface of the board.

You are now prepared for the delineation of figures. With a pair of dividers, take distances from a scale, according to the figure you wish to represent, and transfer the same to paper; and then draw the first outlines with a lead pencil. The pencil lines should extend beyond the angles where the ink lines are to terminate. Having thus defined all the angles with pencil marks, the precise starting point and termination of each ink line will be clearly visible.

After drawing the pencil lines for the whole or a part of a figure, then, with a mathematical drawing pen, trace each line thus drawn, taking care, however, to begin and terminate each ink line at its desired point or angle. The pencil lines may then be erased with India rubber, leaving the figure, with clean angles, drawn in ink.

In drawing an intricate figure, in which a great number of lines are required, it is better to draw only a *part* of it with pencil lines before inking; then proceed again with the pencil, and again with ink, until the whole is completed.

SHADING.—Objects may be better represented by shading the delineations; but this is a more difficult art than drawing lines. Draughtsmen of but limited experience often spoil a well-executed delineation, by a bungling attempt at shading. It is highly important to the beginner to be familiar with certain principles in theory, before he attempts to *practice* in the art of drawing. Experience is but a dull teacher when unassisted by theory.

Let the student carefully observe the following directions:

First, delineate a plain figure like Fig. 3 or Fig. 4, on Plate V. Then prepare the color for the lights. Let the strength of the color be tested by applying it to a piece of waste paper, observing, when it is dry, that it is neither too light nor too dark. Then take a sable

brush, and, commencing at a proper point or angle of the figure,
spread the color evenly over the surface, keeping within the outlines
of the figure, and passing as rapidly as convenient to the end or part
of the figure opposite to the point of commencement.   The brush
should be kept well filled, so that the ink may be made to flow evenly
over the surface as represented in the Figures.   It is made very
evident in the Figures, that the artist suspended his work with a
sufficient supply of ink to spread over the entire surface.   But the
student, instead of stopping as there represented, should continue
his operations until he has reached the outlines of the surface to be
shaded; and should he find an excess of ink at the point where he
has last used the brush, let him extract the ink from his brush, and
sponge up the surplus liquid, leaving the surface of a uniform color.
He should never attempt to dispose of this excess of color by brush-
ing back on the surface already finished and partially dry, nor should
he touch the brush to any part of the surface over which he has
once passed, as it will deepen the color upon every spot thus re-
touched, and spoil the drawing.

The student should first practice shading on plain figures, until
he can hold the brush steadily, and trace the surface outlines accu-
rately.   Let him then commence shading in projection, as seen in
Fig. 2.

The simplest and most common rule in shading the projection
from surfaces, is to make the depth of the shade equal to the projection of the object, as may be seen by the Figure.   The surface to
be shaded may be first delineated with pencil lines; and then, with a
dark color, pass over the surface as above directed, holding the
brush as a pen is held in writing.

If the shade is not found to be sufficiently dark by passing once over a figure, let the operation be repeated once or twice, until the proper depth of shade is obtained. Indeed, it is better to pass over the dark shades two or three times, as it will prevent the work from having a spotted appearance. It should be observed, that the *lights* are first made over the entire surface before commencing at the *shades.*

In shading an elevation, or any figure delineated by a large number of lines, it is necessary, after a sufficient quantity of color is prepared, to commence shading by selecting a single division or simple figure in the design, bounded by lines, and completing that before proceeding farther. For instance, we are to shade Fig. 1, on Plate V, we shall commence at one end of the cornice, passing over the facia and crown mould, before touching the frieze. And thus proceed, taking up divisions separately, until the whole is completed— that is, till the light tint is finished—after which, the shading of projections can be undertaken. It is sometimes best to make the light tint, on an elevation, before the windows are delineated, as it is difficult to color the walls and keep to the boundaries of all the windows, without some part of the unfinished work becoming dry before renewing the operation with the brush. But if the walls of the house are first tinted, it should be with a light color, as a dark tint would injure the final coloring of the windows.

PLATE I.

GEOMETRICAL DEFINITIONS.

1. GEOMETRY is the science which has for its object the measurement of extension.

Extension has three dimensions—length, breadth, and height, or thickness.

2. A *line* is length without breadth or thickness.

The extremities of a line are called points; a point, therefore, has neither length, breadth, nor thickness, but position only.

3. A *straight line* is the shortest distance from one point to another.

4. Every line which is not straight, or composed of straight lines, is a *curved line*.

The word *line*, when used alone, will designate a straight line; and the word *curve*, a curved line.

5. A *surface* is that which has length and breadth, without height or thickness.

6. A *plane* is a surface, in which, if two points be assumed at pleasure, and connected by a straight line, that line will lie wholly in the surface.

7. A *solid*, or *body*, is that which has length, breadth, and thickness; and, therefore, combines the three dimensions of extension.

When two straight lines meet each other, as in 3, their inclination or opening is called an *angle*, which is greater or less, as the lines are more or less inclined or opened. The point of intersection is called the vertex of the angle, and the straight lines its sides.

9. When a straight line meets another straight line, so as to make the adjacent lines equal to each other, as in 1, each of these angles is called a *right angle.*

10. Every angle less than a right angle, is an *acute angle;* and every angle greater than a right angle, is an *obtuse angle.*

11. Two lines are said to be *parallel,* when situated in the same plane, as 4, they cannot meet, how far soever, either way, both of them be produced.

12. A *plane figure* is a plane terminated on all sides by lines, either straight or curved. If the lines are straight, the space they enclose is called a *rectalineal figure,* or *polygon,* and the lines themselves, taken together, form the *contour,* or *perimeter* of the polygon.

13. The polygon of three sides, the simplest of all, is called a *triangle;* that of four sides, a *quadrilateral;* that of five, a *pentagon;* that of six, a *hexagon;* that of seven, a *heptagon;* that of eight, an *octagon;* that of nine, a *nonagon;* that of ten, a *decagon;* and that of twelve, a *dodecagon.*

14. An *equilateral triangle* is one which has its three sides equal; an *isosceles* triangle, one with two of its sides equal; a *scalene* triangle, one which has its three sides unequal. The three forms are represented in 5, 6, and 7, on the Plate.

15. A *right-angled triangle* is one which has a right angle. The side opposite the right-angle is the *hypothenuse.*

16. Among the quadrilaterals are

The *square,* represented in 10, which has its sides equal and its angles right angles.

The *rectangle,* in 9, its angles right angles, without having its sides equal.

The *parallelogram*, or *rhomboid*, in 12, which has its opposite sides parallel.

The *rhombus*, or *lozenge*, in 11, which has its sides equal, without having its angles right angles.

And the *trapezoid*, in 14, only two of whose sides are parallel.

A *tangent*, as in 15, is a straight line touching a circle.

To bisect, or divide a given line into two parts: Let 1 2 (Fig. 1,) be the given line. From the points 1 2, as centers, with any distance in your dividers greater than half and less than the whole of the line 1 2, for a radius, as 1 4, and 2 3, describe arcs cutting each other at 5 and 6. Then draw the line 5 6, and the line 1 2 is bisected at 7.

To find the length or stretch-out of the segment of a circle: Let 1 2 3, (Fig. 2,) be a given arc. Draw the chord 1 3; bisect the given arc in 2; then, with 1 as a center, and 1 2 as a radius, describe the arc 2 6. Produce the chord 1 2; then with the distance 1 2 or 1 6 in your dividers, placing one leg on 6, make 4 6 equal to 1 6; then divide 4 3 into three equal parts; add to 6 4 one of the three parts (found in dividing 3 4) to 1 4, and the line 1 5 will be the stretchout of the arc 1 2 3.

To find the stretch-out of a semicircle: Let 1 6 2, (Fig. 3,) be the semicircle. Draw the chord 1 2; then with one foot of your dividers in 1, and the distance 1 2 for a radius, describe an arc at 3. With one foot of your dividers in 2, with the distance 2 1 for a radius, describe an arc cutting the other arc at 3. Then join 3 1 and 3 2, thus making 1 2, 2 3, and 3 1, an equilateral triangle. Then parallel to 1 2 draw the tangent 5 6 4, touching the arc at 6, and produce the line 3 2 to 4, and the line 3 1 to 5. The distance 5 4 will then be the stretch-out of the semicircle 1 6 2.

To Produce a Square equal to two given Squares: Let 1 5 and 2 4 (Fig. 4) be the given squares. Draw the diagonal line 3 4; then form a square by making each of its sides equal to the diagonal lines 3 4, as 3 4, 4 7, 7 6, and 6 3; or,

Place one of each of the given sides at right angles to each other, and square the hypothenuse. The square thus formed will be equal to the two given squares.

To make an Ellipsis with a Trammel: Let 1 3 and 2 4, (Fig. 5,) be the two diameters of the required ellipsis. Let 6 7 8 be a trammel, 6 being the point for a pencil, and 7 8 places for pins to move in grooves. Make 6 7 equal to half of the shortest diameter, by moving the heads which contain the pins and pencil, which may be adjusted by means of screws similar to the common gauge head. Then make 6 8 equal to half of the longest diameter; that is, equal to 1 5; then, by moving the trammel while the pins 7 8 are in the grooves, an ellipsis will be described with the pencil 6, as seen by the Figure.

Fig. 6 shows a method of describing an arch for a bridge.

It should be here remarked, that in many situations where arches are necessary, the span is so great that the segment cannot be described with a trammel, or rod, by reason of the great distance from the centre to the circumference. It will be necessary, therefore, to observe the following directions before the diagram is explained:

We will suppose we are to erect a bridge of 100 feet span, and that we are to construct timber arches, that will rise ten feet in the highest point of the arch. We will first draw a plan of the bridge on a small scale, representing the entire arch of the timbers. We will then divide the arch into a number of segments convenient for practical purposes—say the whole arch into four segments, giving twenty-five feet to each. We shall then draw a chord line in the segment, to ascertain the spring of the twenty-five feet segment; after which, we will apply the rule here given in Fig. 6:

On one edge of the timber make the line 3 1 4, Fig. 6. Make 3 4 equal to the chord found in the segment of the arch. Bisect 3 4 at 1. Raise the perpendicular line 1 6 2, and make 1 2 equal to the spring of the arch in the segment of twenty-five feet. Drive pins in 4, 3 and 2. Bisect 1 2 at 6, and draw 6 3 and 2 3. Produce 6 3 to 5. Draw 2 5, making it equal to 2 3. Then 2 5 6 3 is the form of a board with which to describe the segment of the arch. This is done by placing a pencil at the obtuse angle 2, making it fast by means of a staple, and moving the board longitudinally, keeping the edge against the pins.

PLATE II.

Fig. 1 represents an elevation of an upper gable window, designed for a stone or brick cottage. The cap is designed to be of dressed stone, with a joint in the center. The sill is also of dressed stone.

Fig. 2 exhibits the plan of Fig. 1, with a portion of the brick wall in W W. *o o o* Shows the sash jambs. *c c c c c c c c* Shows a section of the sash stiles. *u u u* Exhibits the inside jamb.

Fig. 4 represents an elevation of an inside door casing, with a cornice head supported at the ends by small consoles.

Fig. 3 represents a section of the cornice, *y* showing a section of the crown mould, *k* the facia, *g* the planceer, and *o* the bed mould.

PLATE III.   55

Fig. 5 shows a plan of Fig. 4, with a horizontal section of the studs *s s, s s*. *t t* Shows a section of the door jambs, and *c c* the face casing.

Fig. 6 is a side view of the console seen in Fig. 4.

The subjoined scale will measure any of the Figures on this Plate, with the exception of Fig. 3, which is measured by the scale accompanying it

---

PLATE III.

Fig. 1, on this Plate, is an example of an ante and entablature. The height and projection of the several members in this and the other designs on the Plate, are designated by minutes in the column of figures at the left hand of each design.

Fig. 4 is the section of the cornice for Fig. 1. C shows the bracket or cornice block, *h* the crown mould, *t* the facia, *x* the planceer, and *i* the bed mould.

Fig. 2 is an example for an entablature, and Fig. 5 exhibits a section of the cornice seen in Fig. 2. *y* Is the crown mould, *h* the facia, *x* the planceer, and *i t* the bed mould.

Fig. 3 is an example for an Ionic cornice suitable for brick or stone buildings, and for all buildings upon which it is improper or inconvenient to employ the entire entablature.

Fig. 6 shows a section of the cornice seen in Fig. 3. *b* Is the crown mould, *y* the facia, *x* the planceer, *i* the upper member in the bed mould, and *h* the lower member in the bed mould. *q* Shows a section of the bed for the dentils, and *t* exhibits the dentils.

PLATE IV.

On Plate IV are two designs for base, and one for windows and doors.

Fig. 1 shows an inside elevation of a window, the plan of which is seen in Fig. 2.

F is the panel below the window.

S S S S, the studding.

C C, face casing.

G G, band moulds.

R, lath and plastering.

O, a section of a design for base.

The accompanying scale measures any part of Fig. 1 and Fig. 2.

Fig. 3 is a design for a base drawn at half size.

Fig. 4 is a section of the face casing seen in Fig. 1. This Figure is also drawn at half size.

This style of finish is very common, and most builders are familiar with it. It will answer a good purpose in many situations.

PLATE V.

Fig. 1 is a design for a Grecian Ante and Entablature, though it is not of Grecian example. The entablature, being of few members, was more particularly designed for a figure by which to explain and illustrate the scale of minutes, or scale of proportions, in drawing the Grecian Orders, which is given in another place, under the

PLATE VI. 57

head of "Scale of Minutes." Yet, the capital is a very good design for an ante cap. The entablature will answer a tolerable purpose in many situations, particularly where cheap and plain work is desired.

Fig. 2 illustrates the depth of shade in architectural representations, which, however, is more particularly explained under the head of "Primary Rules for Drawing." Figs. 3 and 4 are explained under the same head.

PLATE VI.

Figs. 3 and 4, on Plate VI, represent the two opposite sides of the common plain scale, or scale of equal parts.

Each number in the column of figures at the left hand on Fig. 4, designate the fractional part of an inch contained in one of the small divisions set opposite of the same on the scale. Thus, one of the small divisions opposite of the number 20, contains one-twentieth part of an inch; opposite 25, one-twenty-fifth part of an inch; and so on to 45. Each of the wider spaces, reading from left to right, 1, 2, 3, 4, &c., is equal to the ten *small* divisions on each respective line.

On paper, these scales are made to answer the purposes of scales of proportion in most of the branches of mathematical drawing. In land measure, the divisions are used as chains and links. In architecture, they are sometimes used as minutes in drawing the orders, and sometimes as feet and inches.

The series of small divisions on Fig. 4, reading from C, 10, 20, 30, 40, 50, 60, 70, 80, 90, is a scale of chords, the use of which is to lay out and measure angles.   What is meant by measuring an angle, is ascertaining, in degrees, minutes, &c., of a circle, the distance between two straight lines diverging from a common point.   Every circumference, great or small, contains 360 degrees; and every quarter circle contains, therefore, 90 degrees in the arch of the two radii, as seen in Fig. 1.   The perpendicular line 60 90, is one radius, and the horizontal line A 60, the other; which form the angle A 60 and 60 90, an angle of 90 degrees, known also as a right angle.   This may be made clearer by referring again to Fig. 1, Plate VI, where it will be seen that the perpendicular line rising from 60 to 90 is at an angle of 90 degrees with the horizontal plane A 60, and a straight line drawn from 60 on the horizontal plane, to 40 on the arch, would produce an angle of 40 degrees from the plane.   Again, a line drawn from 60 on the plane, to 20 on the arch, would produce an angle of 20 degrees.

A scale of chords, as seen on Fig. 4 at C, are found by dividing a quadrant of a circle into 90 parts, as seen in Fig. 1, where it will be perceived that the entire length of the horizontal plane A 90, is equal to the chord of the arch, or a straight line drawn from A to 90 and a straight line drawn from A to 80, on the arch, is equal to A 80 on the plane, making A 80 on the plane the chord of A 80 on the arch; thus dividing each of the 9 divisions on the arch into 10 equal parts, as seen at A 10; and with one leg of the dividers placed on A, transfer from the arch each of the 90 divisions to the horizontal plane A 90, as seen by the dotted lines, 90 90, 80 80, and so on to the completion of the scale.

To lay out an angle by a scale of chords: Take the distance C 60 on Fig. 4, with a pair of dividers, and with this distance for a radius, place one leg of the dividers on the point from which you

PLATE VI. 59

wish to raise an angle, and with the other leg, holding a pencil, describe the quadrant of a circle; then place one foot of the dividers on C, Fig. 4, and extend the other to any desired angle, and transfer the distance thus obtained to the arch last described; then, lines drawn from those two points in the arch to the center from which the arch was drawn, will be the desired angle. For instance: We seek an angle of 30 degrees. Take the distance C 30, Fig. 4, and transfer it to the arch, from which draw lines to the center, and the angle formed by the meeting of the lines is an angle of 30 degrees. And thus any desired angle may be obtained. It should be observed, that the arch first described should always have for its radius the distance C 60 on the scale of chords.

In measuring angles already drawn, take the distance C 60 from the scale of chords, with a pair of dividers, and with this distance as a radius, place one foot of the dividers in the angle to be measured, and with the other describe an arch from the leg to the base of the angle; then, with the dividers, take the distance of the chord of the arch, and apply it to the scale of chords. The distance from C to the other point of the dividers designates the angle of the figure.

Fig. 2 exhibits a method of drawing an octagon within the square 1, 2, 3, 4. Draw the diagonal lines 4 2 and 3 1. Then, with one foot of the dividers in 1, extend the other to the center 13 for a radius, and describe the arch 8, 13, 5. Then, with one foot of the dividers in 2, describe the arch 10, 13, 7; and proceed thus at each of the 4 angles. Then join 6 7, 5 12, 11 10, and 9 8, and the octagon is complete.

PLATE VII.

On Plate VII is a design for a small yet very convenient Cottage. Its arrangements are easily understood by an examination of the ground and chamber plans. The vestibule or hall is 4 feet 6 inches by 9 feet, on the plan, and 9 feet high. The main part is 24 by 31 feet on the plan, and 14 feet high. The wood house part is 15 feet 6 inches, by 10 feet 6 inches, on the plan, and 9 feet high.

The height of the first story is 8 feet 6 inches; the second story is finished to collar-beams, 7 feet above the floor. The size of the several apartments are given in the clear—walls not included—D R, Dining Room; B R, Bed-Room; P, Pantry.

It will be perceived by the ground and chamber plans, and also by the perspective view, that there are but two windows in each end of the main part of the house, one directly over the other. These windows being double or mullion windows, admit of partitions in the center, thus throwing part of the window into one room and part into another. There are four double windows in the first story, each having 16 lights of 9 by 15 glass—one window in the bed room of 12 lights, 9 by 15 glass; one in the pantry of 8 lights, 9 by 12 glass; and 2 in the vestibule of 8 lights, 9 by 15 glass.

In the second story are 2 double windows of 16 lights, 9 by 12 glass; and 2 small windows in the back or rear, of 6 lights, 9 by 15 glass.

In the wood house, it is only designed to have a window over the door. Yet some may choose to have the wood house extended so

PLATE VIII.   61

as to make a kitchen of the present wood room; in which case, 2 windows of 12 lights, 9 by 12 glass, would be needed.

Frame.—The posts should be 5 by 8 inches, and the studding 2 by 5, obviating the necessity of having corners of posts in the angles of rooms. The studding on the side may extend from the sill to the plate; then spike the first joists to every stud, in place of employing girders. The elevation of the roof is necessarily high, for the convenience of the chamber. The ridge should rise 10 or 11 feet above the plate. There should be lap-studs in the gable; also, a few studs in the middle cross partition, both above and below, before putting on the roof, as the combined weight of the rafters, boards, and shingles, would have a tendency to spread the plates. It would also be desirable to mark the place for the collar-beams, on the rafters, when framed, and nail on the collar-beams at the time the rafters are raised.

The finish of this cottage should be plain, yet the builder should exercise some taste in selecting the several designs necessary for the interior.

PLATE VIII.

On Plate VIII is a design for a Farm House. The ground and chamber plans are drawn on a scale half the size of that from which the elevation is drawn.

It will be perceived that this design will make a cheap, but convenient and comfortable residence, for a farmer in moderate circumstances. The form of the outline renders it more suitable as one upon which to employ the bracketed style in its decoration.

Although, if it were necessary to conform to the peculiar notions of those who may prefer it, we may employ a Grecian entablature in place of the bracketed cornice. Yet, if brackets were not used, it would be better to let the entire raking cornice mitre and intersect with the eave cornice, in which case the planceer or soffit of the eave cornice would have an inclination parallel with the rafters or roof, obviating the necessity of using breaks or returns.

DESCRIPTION.

The upright or main part of this building is **25** by **32** feet, on the plan, and 15 feet high, The wing is 19 by 25 feet, on the plan, and 9 feet high. All the lower rooms are 8 feet 6 inches in the clear. The chamber is finished to collar-beams 7 feet six inches above the floor.

The vestibule or hall is 6 feet 6 inches by 8 feet 6 inches, with stairs landing in a hall or corridor, which leads to every apartment above, as may be seen from the chamber plan. The stairs ascend between partitions, yet they are to remain open, as in the case of hand-rail stairs.

The size of the other apartments are given sufficiently intelligible. D R, signifies Dining-Room; K, Kitchen; P, Pantry; B R, Bed-Room; N, Nursery; P, Porch; and C, the door to the Cellar.

Framing.—It is unnecessary to describe the frame to this building in detail. It should be observed, however, that 4 bents will be necessary in the main part—one at each end of the dining-room—for it will be seen that a *middle* bent would interfere with the plan of the house. The beams of these interior bents should be light, as the joists over the parlor and kitchen should run parallel with them,

PLATE VIII.   63

and be framed into girders, resting on the hall and pantry partitions. All the other joists, in both main part and wing, should run at right angles with those last mentioned.

Windows.—The style of the windows, seen in the elevation, will answer a good purpose, even should the style of the cornice be changed as above mentioned.

The windows below should be twelve-lighted, of glass 9 by 16 inches; and those below should be also twelve-lighted, with glass 9 by 14 inches. The frames should be made to receive blinds.

Masonry.—The cellar will extend under the main part only. The chimney in the main part may rise from the foundation, with a fireplace in the kitchen as well as in the parlor. Or, we may erect a frame foundation, and start a stove chimney two feet below the chamber floor, or at least dropped sufficiently below to admit the stovepipes of the parlor and kitchen at a proper distance from the ceiling. In either case, the chimney should be carried up with two flues, and the top constructed according to the representation in the elevation.

Inside Finish.—A suitable parlor casing may be found on Plate XXI, Fig. 3. Parlor base, Plate XXI, Fig. H. Hall casing, the same as the parlor, except with the tablet over the openings omitted. In the dining-room and other apartments, the builder can select such a finish as is suited to his own taste.

Outside Finish.—For the cornice, on the main part, let the rafters project 2 feet over the frieze-board, the end cut perpendicularly; then nail to the under side of the rafters the planceer, to the edge of which, and to the end of the rafters, nail a facia, reaching one inch below the planceer and up to the top of the rafters. To the upper edge of the facia nail the crown mould.

For the raking cornice, let the roof boards extend over the gable rafters, under which nail blocks having the same thickness and projection as those in the eave cornice, and then let the planceer, facia, and crown mould intersect and mitre with the corresponding members in the eave cornice. A suitable bracket for the eave cornice may be found on Plate XX, Fig. 6. It is made of two-inch plank, and a full size pattern may be obtained by observing the explanations of the several figures on Plate XX. The mode of drawing a corresponding bracket for the rake is also there explained.

The projection of the rafters and the blocks in the rake, should be adjusted in such a manner as to receive a planceer board in the eave and raking cornice, of equal width. The projection of the brackets terminate just back of the facia, and the inch which falls below the planceer will rest upon the upper face of the bracket.

In the cornice on the wing, a similar process should be adopted, except that there should be less projection. The thickness of the projecting part of the rafters and cornice blocks, should be one inch less than in those on the main part of the house.

The brackets on the wing will be smaller than those on the main part, but of the same figure; a pattern of which is found in the same manner as the others, by scale No. 2, on Plate XX, and there explained.

A style of window frame is seen in the elevation.

The house may be covered with siding, or with perpendicular boards or planks, and battened as described in the explanations of Plate XXIII.

PLATE IX. 65

PLATE IX.

The several figures on this Plate were designed to be employed in the perspective view seen on Plate **XXXIV**, and are drawn on a scale of one inch to the foot. Hence, an inch divided into twelve equal parts, will make a scale that will measure any figure or parts of a figure sufficiently accurate for a working drawing. *(See Scale.)*

Fig. 1 is an elevation of the pendant, and part of the raking cornice. The shaft of the pendant is made of boards, as seen by Fig. 6.

The bands **A A** are mitred round each end of the shaft, rising half an inch above the upper end, and falling half an inch below the lower end, to receive the spire **B** and the stalactend **C**, as seen by the dotted lines in **A A**.

The stalactend **C** is made by working a plank into a mould, like Fig. 7, and then mitred, as seen in Fig. 8.

The bottom and top of the shaft are made flush, by bradding in a piece of thin stuff.

Fig. 2 is a section of the rafter, as seen at **M**; section of the plate as seen at **D**; section of the roof boards, as seen at **X**; planceer, at **H**; facia, **G**; crown mould, **T**; and wall at **F**.

Fig. 3 is a section of the raking cornice-block **K**, of the facia **R**, of the planceer **V**, and the roof-board **U**.

Fig. 6 shows the plan of the pendant shaft.

Fig. 4 shows the plan of the chimney top, rising through the roof a parallelogram, and then changing into two octagons, **N N**.

Fig. 5 shows an elevation of the chimney flues above the roof.

PLATE X.

On Plate X are two designs for gable cornices, and one design for
a pendant.

Fig. 1 represents a fragment of a design for a gable cornice with
the ornamented barge-board. This design is heavy and is best
calculated for a stone or brick building.

All the figures on this Plate are to be measured from the annexed
scale.

The main member or ground to the barge or frieze, in Fig. 1, is
to be made of two-inch plank, and seen at N. The vine X is to be
made of one and one-half-inch plank, of a semi-ellipsis form, and
attached with screws. The stalactends R R are circular in their
plan, and attached to the main plank and vine with nails. It should
be here observed that this plane, to which the stalactends are
attached, should always be parallel to the horizon, whatever may be
the angle or pitch of the roof.

A section of the eave cornice is seen at Fig 6. e Represents the
rafter; r section of the frieze; w section of the planceer; v section
of the facia; u section of the crown mould; d roof-boards; b eave
gutter; and f the place for the fringe.

Fig. 2 represents another design for a gable fringe, together with
a design for a pendant. It will be observed, in the construction of
this cornice, that the facia is beveled on the lower edge, to which are
attached inverted conic sections, of the same thickness of the facia,
and with a like bevel on the edges. The grounds in which the leaves

PLATE XI.   67

are cut should be one-half-inch thick in the gables of wood buildings, and two inches in those of brick or stone. The pendant in Fig. 2 is clearly illustrated by its elevation and sections; Fig. 4 representing a horizontal section of the shaft, and *k*, Fig. 4, the projection to the cap of the pinnacle.

Fig. 5 shows a plan and section of a design for a stalactend in a pendant.

It will be observed, in Fig. 2, that the pinnacle will require 8 small brackets, 2 on each of its sides. The bud in the panel is a semi-ellipsis in its plan.

PLATE XI.

This Plate comprises three designs for the inside finish of windows and doors.

Fig. 1 represents a fragment of a door or window casing, in which the top moulding in the base intersects and is mitred with the band moulding of the casing, F showing a plan of the face casing and moulding, and Y a section of the base.

The plinth of the base is made flush with the face of the casing. In the grooving of the face casing, at the bottom, a piece is fitted to make a continued plane of the base and casing, as high as the plinth of the base.

The break in the top of the casing is made by cutting away the upper margin the entire depth of the groove, nailing to the upper edge of the casing another margin, which forms the break, as may be seen in the figure.

Fig. 2 represents another design for door and window casing, but differing essentially in its features and construction from the one last described.

A section of the cornice, in this design is seen in Fig. 4. *r* Shows the top casing or frieze, *o* the bed moulding, which is fitted in between the blocks. *n* Shows a section of the blocks, *g* the corona, and *n* the crown moulding. N is the face of the blocks.

Fig. 5 is a plan of the face casing and jamb. *r r* Exhibit sections of semi-columns standing in the elevation upon a paneled plinth. These semi-columns are capped by a rectangular block, over which is placed brackets to support the projection of the cornice. A side view of the bracket may be seen in J. R is a section of a design for base.

Fig. 3 is an elevation for another design for inside casing.

Fig. 6 is a section or plan of the face casing and jamb. *u,* In this Figure, is rabbetted to the thickness of the lath and plaster. The band moulding, *x,* is not to be attached to the ground *u* until the walls are plastered, when it will be extended on to the plastered walls enough to hide the joint.

This Plate was drawn from the accompanying scale.

PLATE XII.

This Plate exhibits three designs for balustrades, intended for balconies and for parapets on the roofs of verandas. A veranda may, sometimes, have a deck roof, with a surrounding balustrade, in which case, the roof becomes a spacious and pleasant balcony.

PLATE XII. 69

In constructing a balustrade on the roof of a veranda, it is necessary to construct the pillars of the balustrade directly over the columns in the veranda.

Fig. 1 represents an elevation of one panel of a design for a balustrade. The panel of this design is made by cutting the small figure out of an inch board of sufficient width, to the top of which is attached a rail having bevel edges, as seen in the figure. The base to the panel is a plank one and one-half inches thick, fastened with screws to the face of the panel. The angular figures on the panel are mitred at each of their four angles, and fastened to the panel with screws. The form of the face of this member is two inclined planes, as may be seen in the Figure.

Fig. 2 is the plan of Fig. 1.

Fig. 3 is of more simple construction. The base is an inch board, fastened to the face of a panel in the same manner as in Fig. 1. At regular intervals on the panel are circular-headed battens joined to the base. Between these battens the panel is opened by cutting out the figures seen in the design.

Fig. 4 is a plan of Fig. 3.

Fig. 5 is constructed very similar to Fig. 1, but differing in design. It should be observed, in this design, that the edges of the openings in the panel are beveled, and also that there is a bottom-rail instead of the plank base.

Fig. 6 is a ground plan of Fig. 5.

The accompanying scale will measure any part of the several figures on this Plate.

PLATE XIII.

On this plate are five designs for veranda columns.

Fig. 1 represents the elevation of a light open column. **A,** in this figure, exhibits a horizontal section. The sides or borders should be attached to the panel by means of screws.

Fig. 4 represents a design of similar character, but with a different device in the panel.

Fig. 5 is constructed somewhat differently, the arches being made of two-inch plank, and attached to the sides before the column is united together. The two sides of the column are united by means of screws passing through the arches where they touch each other. The rosettes are separate figures, and also of two-inch plank, attached by screws from the outside.

E shows a horizontal section of Fig. 5.

Fig. 3 represents a column of quite a different character. The shaft consists of four semicircles, in its plan, as may be seen by its horizontal section at C, where is also seen the plan of the capital.

Fig. 2. The construction of this column is somewhat similar to the open columns, but it will be seen by its plan at **B** that it is made of two-inch plank. The arch, at the top, is made by fitting a block between the borders.

These several designs were drawn, and should be measured, by the subjoined scale.

In designing and constructing verandas with open columns, it will be necessary to observe the general principles and directions in

PLATE XIV. **71**

Fig. 2, Plate XXXVI, where the whole modus operandi is clearly illustrated and explained.

PLATE XIV.

This Plate represents a column and entablature in the Grecian style, but not of Grecian example.

The example here given has many of the features and proportions of the Doric Order, yet is without the triglyphs and mutules, which are important in point of expense in the antique Grecian models.

This entablature and column are very easily executed by builders of ordinary experience. The entablature may be employed in many situations without the columns.

Before any attempt is made to draw and execute this or any other example that is proportioned by a scale of minutes, the student should obtain a thorough knowledge of the scale by studying carefully the article under the head of "Scale of Minutes."

A semi-plan of the top and bottom of the column is shown in the example. This column has no base, and in this respect does not differ from the Grecian model. This is a merit rather than a defect in the Doric Order. The base of a column is often in the way, and not unfrequently becomes defaced; and, when constructed of wood, aids decay. These remarks, however, apply to the Doric column only as it is frequently employed in this country in particular situations, in which they are generally constructed of wood, as in the fronts of porticoes, and in colonades in the fronts of residences.

PLATE XV.

Fig. 1, on this Plate, shows the method of finding the different bevels in a hip-roof.

Let $b\,e\,r\,c$ be the plan of the roof. Bisect $c\,b$ at j and $r\,e$ at s. Draw the line $j\,s$, and take the distance $j\,b$ and set it from j to f on the line $j\,s$. Draw the diagonal lines $f\,b$ and $f\,c$ for the base of the hip rafters.

To find the length and bevel of the common rafter at a quarter pitch: Draw $d\,h\,f$ parallel to $c\,j\,b$. Bisect $d\,f$ at h, and with f for a center, describe the arch $h\,e$. Then draw the line $d\,e$, which will be the length of the rafter, and the bevel seen at e, on the lines $d\,e$ and $e\,f$, is the down mitre.

To find the length and mitre of the hip-rafter: From the base of the hip $f\,b$ erect the perpendicular $f\,a$, making it equal to $f\,e$, as seen by the arc $e\,a$. Then draw the line $a\,b$, which is of the length of the hip-rafter, and the bevel seen at a is the down mitre.

To find the length and bevel of the jack-rafters: With b for a center from a, describe an arc to intersect the line $j\,s$ at g, and from this point of intersection draw the diagonal lines $g\,b$ and $g\,c$; and then parallel to $f\,j$ draw the lines $1\,2\,3\,4\,5\,6\,7$, extending from the line $j\,b$ to the diagonal line $g\,b$, thereby determining the length of each of the jack-rafters. The angle at g, made by the lines $g\,j$ and $g\,b$ is the face or top mitre. The down mitre will be the same as in the common rafter seen by the bevel at e.

PLATE XV.   **73**

To find the face or top bevel to the hip-rafter: Make *r l*, in **A**, equal to *f j*, in **B**, and from *l* draw *l a c* parallel with *r s e*, in **A**. Then draw the base lines *a r* and *a e*, and make *a d*, in **A**, equal to *f e* in **B**; and draw *d l*. Erect the perpendicular *a* 4, making it equal to *a d*, as seen by the arc *d* 4. Draw 4 *e*, and produce the base line *e a* to *q*. Draw the diagonal lines *q s* and *q c*. Then set off half the width of the hip-rafter on each side of the center, and draw the parallel lines as seen at 2 and 3. The angle then seen at *q* is the face mitre of the hip-rafter.

To find the backing to the hip-rafter: At right angle with the base line *a e*, draw *g j f;* and from *n*, on the line 4 *e*, draw *n j* perpendicular to 4 *e*. Make *j h* equal to *j n*. Draw the lines *h g* and *h f*, and the angle seen at *h* will be the back of the hip-rafter.

To find the bevel for a purlin joining the hip-rafter: At right angle with the pitch of the roof *d l* draw a section of the purlin, as seen at *w*. Draw 9 *o k* parallel with *l a c*, and make *o k* and *o* 9 equal to *o m*, as may be seen by the arcs *m k* and 9 *x*. Draw *k h* and *m a* parallel with the line *d s*. At right angle with the line *h k* draw *h a*, meeting *m a* at the point of intersection with *a r*. Draw *o p*, *x v* and 9 *t* parallel with *k h*. At right angle with *x v* draw *v t*. Then from *t* draw *t p* for the face or top bevel, and *h p* for the down bevel, as seen by the figure of the bevels at *p*.

Figs. 2 and 3 show a method of finding the curve in a hip-rafter for a concave roof.

Let the straight line **A** *d*, Fig. 3, be the span of the roof, and the two parallel curved lines **A** *d*, a section or side view of the rafter. Draw **A E** at right angle with the straight line **A** *d*, and make **A E** equal to **A** *d*, Fig. 3. Draw the diagonal line **E** *d*, Fig. 2, for the base of the hip. Then draw lines from the top of, in Fig 3, parallel with the line E A until they intersect the base of the hip E *d*, Fig. 2; then, from the points of intersection, erect ordinates of any convenient length perpendicular to E *d*.

Take the distance *d d*, Fig. 3, and make *d d*, Fig. 2. Take the distance *c c*, Fig. 3, and make *c c*, Fig. 2; and thus proceed until the top curve in Fig. 2 is completed.

For the convex or under edge of the rafter, proceed in a similar manner, by taking the distance to the under edge of the rafter in Fig. 3, and making the under edge of the hip-rafter in Fig. 2.

Fig. 4 is an example for a Grecian cornice, in which is shown a method for mitring an inclined planceer.

Let *d b*, Fig. 4, be the width and inclination of the board to be mitred; draw the horizontal line *b e;* and then the perpendicular line *d e a*, and make *e a* equal to *e b*, as seen by the arc *b a*. On *d* for a centre, and *d b* for a radius, describe the arc *b f;* then drop the perpendicular *f g*, and, from *a*, draw *a g* parallel with *e b*, and the diagonal line *g e* will be the required mitre.

Fig. 5 shows a method of finding a raking mould that will mitre with the eave mould, and also a horizontal mould to mitre with the rake at the top.

Let 1 2 3 4 5 6, at A, be the flexure of the eave mould, and D I the upper edge of the fillet. Let fall from D I the perpendicular 1 2 3 4 5 6 to G. From D draw the pitch of the roof D B F, and, parallel to it, draw G H and all the intermediate lines from the profile of the eave 1 2 3 4 5 6. Parallel with D I, and from the point of intersection between the raking lines and eave mould, draw the horizontal lines 2 2, 3 3, 4 4, 5 5, and 6 6. Then at B draw the line at right angle with D B F. Take the distance 1 1, on the eave mould, and make 1 1 at B; take the distance 2 2, on the eave mould,

PLATE XVI. 75

and make **2 2** on the rake at **B**; and thus proceed until the raking mould is complete.

The horizontal mould at **H C F** is found by taking the same distances from the eave mould and making **1 2 3 4 5 6**, on the horizontal line, seen at **F**, and dropping perpendicular lines to each corresponding line in the rake, and then tracing the curve through each point of intersection, as may be seen in the Figure.

PLATE XVI.

On this Plate are two designs for entablatures and one for a cornice. The entablatures may be used with or without columns and antes.

The cornice, Fig. 3, should never be employed in connection with columns or antes, as it is indispensable in the use of the Grecian style to place columns and antes under a full entablature.

Either of these examples are good designs for inside stucco cornices, and, in some situations, may be employed with the whole entablature; in others, to the top of the architrave only.

To proportion these designs for room cornices, it will be necessary to observe the same rules as those used in the proportion of outside entablatures; that is, find a scale of minutes from the height of the room.

PLATE XVII.

This Plate shows the method of drawing and constructing the Ionic capital and column.

Fig. 1 exhibits an elevation of the capital, and a semi-plan of the column.

Fig. 4 is a plan of the column and the under side of the capital. A A show the projection of the abacus, seen in the elevation at N; *b b b b*, the convex edges of the volutes; *d d d d*, the flanks of the capital; *c c c c*, the eyes of the volutes, seen at H H in the elevation; *e*, the echinus, seen at *e* in the elevation; *f*, the astragal, seen at *f* in the elevation; and *g*, the apophyge, or curve which serves to connect the capital with the shaft of the column.

To draw the Ionic Volutes: Draw the horizontal line at the top of the volutes, Fig. 1.   Make *y y* 54 minutes.   Drop the perpendicular line *y j d* H, and make *y* H 20 minutes, for the center of the eye at H, Fig. 1.   Draw twelve centers for describing the volutes.   These centers are drawn, as represented, by enlarged centers in Fig 2, H, Fig. 2, being the center of the eye as seen at H, Fig. 1.   Make H N, and H 9, Fig. 2, each one and one-quarter minutes.   At N and 9 draw the horizontal lines 9 10 and N 11 at right angles with N H 9.   Make N 11 and 9 10 each one and one-half minutes, and join 10 11.   Draw the diagonal lines H 10 and H 11.   Produce 11 N to 12, and make N 12 one minute.   Divide the diagonal lines H 10 and H 11 each into three equal parts, at

PLATE XVII.   77

2 6 and 3 7. Join 2 3 and 6 7, and, parallel to N 11, draw the lines 7 8, 3 4, 2 1, and 6 5, and the centers for drawing the volutes will be complete.

We will now suppose these centers to be drawn at H, Fig. 1. Then, from H, as a center, draw the eye 7 minutes in diameter. Then place one foot of the dividers on 1, as a center, extending the other to the top of the eye, and describe a quarter circle; then place one foot of the dividers on 2, as a centre, extending the other to the termination of the quarter circle last described, and describe the arc 11 10; then, with 3 for a center, describe the arc 10 9; with 4 for a center, describe the arc 9 8; with 5, describe 8 7; with 6, describe 7 6; with 7, describe 6 5; with 8, describe 5 4; with 9, describe 4 3; with 10, describe 3 2; with 11, describe 2 1; and with 12, describe 1 y, which will complete the convex side of the hem.

The hem is drawn and diminished in the following manner: Make y j, Fig. 1, 2 minutes. Then draw the perpendicular line A B, Fig. 3, and make the horizontal line, at B, equal to y f, Fig. 1. Then draw the converging line to A, and divide A B into 12 equal parts, as seen in the figure, 1 2 3 4, &c. Then, as the upper line, at B, Fig. 3, is equal to y f, Fig. 1, take the next shorter line at 1, Fig. 3, and make a from 1, Fig. 1; then take the distance of the line next still shorter, at 2, Fig. 3, and make 2 b, Fig. 1; then take 3, Fig, 3, and make 3 c, Fig. 1; and thus proceed until the points are made for the 12 quarter circles of the volute. Now, place one foot of the dividers in 12, it being the center from which 1 y was drawn, and extend the other to j, Fig. 1. With the distance thus taken in the dividers, for a radius, move the foot in, until the other point will describe the arc *j a;* then, with **11 a** as a radius, place the foot to describe *a b;* then with **10 b** as a radius, describe *b c;* and thus proceed, until the concave side of the hem is complete.

A profile of the face of the volutes may be seen at S S, Fig. 1.

The diameter of the column at the top, is 50 minutes, and is, therefore, 4 minutes less in diameter than the distance from the center of one eye to the center of the other.

PLATE XVIII.

This Plate shows a method of obtaining the different lines in a continued hand-railing, and also the method of finding a pattern for the cylinder or well-hole. There is also on this Plate the upper part of a newel-post, with a cap showing the profile of the mould in the rail, and likewise the easing which joins the cap to the straight part of the rail.

The lines here given for finding the face and falling moulds, may, perhaps, appear at first exceedingly complex, but, by a little care and study, the student will find the method very simple and easily to be understood. It should be observed, that the rule here given for finding the falling mould, will give the length of the balusters on the landing precisely equal to that of the long balusters on the stairs, and this without any regard to the diameter of the well-hole. This adds much to the intricate appearance of the figure.

Draw the line *f u e*, Fig. 1, and with *u n* for a radius, describe the inside of the cylinder seen by the dotted semicircle *n n n*. Then, as the face of the balusters must be on the same line with the

PLATE XVIII. 79

face of the string-board and inner face of the cylinder, we will des-cribe the semicircle *h h h*, and make the distance *u h* equal to half the diameter of the balusters at the bottom. The semicircle *h h h* is the centre of the rail. Set off from *h*, on the line *f u e*, half of the size of the rail at *f*, and with *u* for a centre, describe the semi-circle *f g e* for the outside of the rail; then describe the inside of the rail *j j j*. At right angle with *f u e* draw *f* 12, *j* 13, *j* 8, and *e* 6, and cut off 12 13 and 8 6 four inches from the line *f u e* for a straight part of the rail. Now, 12 *f g e* 6 and 13 *j j j* 8, is a hori-zontal plan of the rail.

To find the outside falling mould: Parallel to *f u e*, Fig. 1, draw *a g b*, touching the outside of the rail at *g;* then, with the distance *f e* for a radius, describe the arcs *f c* and *e c;* then draw the straight line *c f* and produce it to *a.* Draw the line *c e* and produce it to *b;* and the line *a g b* will be the stretch-out of the semicircle *f g e.*

Next find the stretch-out of the centre of the rail, by the same process employed for the outside. Taking *h h*, on the line *f u e*, for a radius, find the point *k*, and draw the line *w h* 9 parallel to *a g b*, touching the centre of the rail at *h*. From the point *k* draw *k h* 9 and *k h w;* and *w h* 9 is the stretch-out of the centre of the rail *h h h*.

Drop a perpendicular line from *w h* 9, at *w*, and make *w v* equal to one riser. Then draw a horizontal line at right angle with the perpendicular line *v w*, and make *v r* equal to one step or tread of the stairs. Join *r* and *w;* and *w v r* will be the pitch-board, and *w r* the pitch or rake of the rail. On *w h* 9, at *h*, set up half the altitude of a riser at *y*, and draw *y* 14 parallel to *a g b*. Produce *y* 14 and *r w* until they meet at *x;* then drop a perpendicular line from *x* to *w h* 9 at *s*.   Draw the line *s k*, and, from *u*, draw *i t l*, cutting *s k* at the point where *s k* cuts the centre of the rail *h h h* at *t*.

Then *x y* 14 will be half the altitude of a riser above *w h* 9. We must, therefore, make the outside falling mould the same height at every point, converging to the centre *u*, for which purpose the line *u i t l* is drawn.

From *c* Fig. 1, draw the line *c* 17, cutting the outside of the rail at *l;* then, from 17, and perpendicular to *a g b*, draw the line to *m*, Fig. 3.   Let *m*, Fig. 3, be a convenient distance from Fig. 1 for drawing Fig. 2.   Take the distance *s x*, on Fig. 1, which is half the riser, and set it from *m*, Fig. 3, on the line *m* 17 at 18.   Parallel to *a* 17 *g b*, draw *z* 18 15, and erect the perpendicular lines *a z* and *b* 15.   Join *z* and *m*.   Produce *a g b* to 22 on the right, and 19 on the left, each extension being equal to 12 *f*, Fig. 1, which is the straight part of the rail.   From 19 erect the perpendicular dotted line 19 20 8, and *a z*, Fig. 3, parallel with the pitch of the rail *r w x*, Fig. 1.   Then, from 22 erect the perpendicular dotted line to 21, Fig. 3.   From *m*, and parallel with the line *z* 18 15, draw *m q* and produce it to 21.   Then take the distance *z* 18, Fig. 3, and set it from *m*, on *m q*, at *a*.   Divide *z m* and *m a* into a convenient number of parts constituting points from which to draw ordinates to form the curve or easing to the outside falling mould.

It will be seen that the distance *z m* is greater than the distance *m a*, yet *m a* must have the same number of divisions of *z m*.

Now, by setting off the thickness or depth of the rail, the falling mould is complete.

To draw the inside falling mould: Find the stretch-out of the semicircle *j j j*, Fig. 1, by the same process given for finding

PLATE XVIII. 81

the outside mould, and it will be seen that the tangent 5 *j* 4 is the stretch-out of the semicircle *j j j*.

Now, as before, draw 5 *p*, Fig. 1, cutting *u i t l* and *j j j* at *i*. From *p*, Fig. 1, draw the perpendicular line touching *p*, Fig. 2. Then from *p*, Fig. 2, draw the horizontal line *p* 3, and produce it to *r*, and make 3 *r*, Fig. 2, equal to 12 *f*, Fig. 1. From 3, on the line 5 *j* 4, Fig. 1, erect the perpendicular 5 6, Fig. 2. From 4, on the line 5 *j* 4, Fig. 1, erect the perpendicular 4 3, Fig. 2. Now take the distance *q* 15, Fig. 3, and set it from 3 to *o*, Fig. 2, on the perpendicular line 4 3. Draw the horizontal line *o* 6, Fig. 2, until it meets the perpendicular line 5 6 at 6. Then join 6 and *p*, Fig. 2. Draw 6 7, Fig. 2, parallel with *r w x*, Fig. 1, and make 6 7, Fig. 2, equal to *z* 8, Fig. 3, drawing the ordinates as in the outside falling mould, and setting off the thickness of the rail, when the inside falling mould will be complete.

To find the face mould: Let F E D *g i j* C, Fig. 6, be the semi-plan of the rail, as in Fig. 1. Draw the line *t h*, Fig. 6. Then, parallel with *t h*, draw 1 2 9, touching the corner of the rail at 2. From this line, as a base, erect the perpendicular 9 *g k*, touching the rail piece at *g*. Draw *k* D 1 parallel with the base line 1 2 9, and erect the perpendicular 1 F 1, touching the corner of the rail piece at F, and meeting *k* D 1 at 1. Take the pitch-board *r v w*, Fig. 1, and apply it to 1 D *k*, Fig. 6, by placing the angle *r* on 1 and *v* on the line 1 D *k*. Then, by the edge of the pitch-board *r w* draw the diagonal line 1 2 3 4 5, &c., producing it to 9, on the perpendicular line 9 *g k* 9, Fig. 7. Through *h*, Fig. 6, draw the perpendicular line 8 *h* 8 until it meets the diagonal line at 8, Fig. 7; and through *i*, Fig. 6, erect the perpendicular 7 *i* 7, till it meets the diagonal line at 7. Through *j* draw 4 *j* 4, Fig. 6, to 4,

Fig. 7. Through E draw 3 3 3, and from the resting point C draw 2 2 2. Then draw 5 *a* 5 to 5, and 6 *b* 6 to 6. At right angles with the diagonal line 1 9, Fig. 7, draw ordinates of any convenient length, from each of the points 1 2 3 4, &c. Now, with a pair of dividers, take the distance 9 *g*, Fig. 6, and make 9 9, Fig. 7. Then, with the distance 8 8, Fig. 6, make 8 8, Fig. 7; and so on, until the outside of the face mould is complete. For the inside, on the base line, 1 2 9, Fig. 6, take 7 *i* and make 7 *j*, Fig. 7. Take 6 *b*, Fig. 6, and make 6 *b*, Fig. 7; and proceed thus until the inside is complete. Then join *j* and 9, Fig. 7, for the middle joint of the rail, and 2 and 1 for the other.

Directions for applying the moulds : The plank for a rail piece should be three and one-half inches thick, with one edge square with the face. Then apply the face mould to one side of the plank by placing the inner corners, 2 *j*, flush with the edge of the plank; and then trace the entire edge of the pattern, the ends for joints included. With the pitch-board for a bevel, applied to the edge of the plank, placing *w r*, Fig. 1, flush with the side of the plank and *w* at the point *j*, in Fig. 7, and trace the edge of the pitch board *w v*, on the edge of the plank, and apply the face mould on the other side, placing *j* at the termination of the diagonal mark made by the pitch-board from *j* across the edge of the plank. Now trace the edge of the face mould as before directed for the first side. Then work to the line thus made by the face mould, and apply the inside and outside falling moulds, taking care to place them exactly opposite to each other.

The face mould for the other rail piece will be traced by the edge of the semi-plan F E D *g i j* C, and squared across the edge of the plank; and again placing the pattern on the opposite side—

PLATE XVIII.   83

directly opposite to where it was placed on the top side—and tracing the edges as before. Then work to the mark, both on the sides and ends.

It is better to have the two rail pieces joined with a rail screw joint, after they are worked to the face mould. Then apply the falling mould.

To find a pattern for the cylinder: From the stretch-out of the dotted semicircle, first drawn in Fig. 1, erect the perpendicular 23 C, Fig. 4, and draw the horizontal line C 16 3 to any convenient distance at the right for a part of the gallery skirting. Then from 2 on the stretch-out of the cylinder, Fig. 1, erect the perpendicular to meet the horizontal line c 16 3, Fig. 4, in 3. Then erect the perpendicular from u, Fig. 1, to 16, Fig. 4. Make c b, Fig. 4, equal to one riser, and draw the horizontal b a, making it equal to one tread. Make 16 4, Fig. 4, equal to the depth of the joists or gallery timbers, allowing it to fall enough below to receive the lath and plastering. Then draw 4 1 parallel with c 16 3, Fig. 4. From 4 draw the raking line 4 k w, Fig. 4, parallel with r w on the pitch-board, Fig. 1. Divide 4 k and 4 1 into an equal number of parts, from which draw ordinates to produce the curve or easing. Then 1 k c 3 will be the pattern by which to mark the inside of the cylinder, formed, as it should be, of staves glued together.

k w u, Fig. 4, show the width of the string-board that will just conform to the cylinder, and 3 1 the width of the straight part of gallery skirting, which will also agree in width with the cylinder.

Fig. 5 shows a newel cap and easing, drawn on a scale of one-sixth of an inch to the inch. It is, therefore, one-sixth of its full size The other Figures on the Plate are drawn from the same scale.

PLATE XIX.

On this Plate is a design for a Cottage residence, in the Italian style.

The arrangements of the several apartments, both in the first and second stories, are delineated with sufficient clearness, in the ground and chamber plans, to need no further description. The ground and chamber plans were drawn from the annexed scale; the elevation from one twice as large. Thus, in measuring the elevation by the scale here given, it will be necessary to take two feet for one, or to make a scale of twice the size.

A better design for a console than is here represented, may be found on Plate XX. The design seen at Fig. 8, Plate XX, is very suitable for a house of this character. A design, with details, for a veranda, suitable for the house given in Plate XIX, should be selected from Plate XXXV, where are several designs for verandas for buildings of a similar construction. That in Fig. 8 would be appropriate for this cottage.

Inside Finish.—A suitable finish for windows and doors, both for the parlor and dining room, may be found on Plate XXI; and also a corresponding style of base at N on the same Plate. In the finish of the other apartments, the builder can consult his own taste, though he should not depart from the general character of style as above given.

For the construction of the sliding doors between the parlor and

PLATE XX.   85

dining room, I would recommend the plan seen in Figs. 4 and 5, on Plate XXI.

This design may be constructed of stone or brick, but in the engraving it is represented with rubble stone walls, with cut stone corners. However, it may be constructed of wood, and yet make a good appearance.

PLATE XX.

On this Plate are eight designs for brackets and consoles. Fig. 1 represents the side and front view of a console of peculiar construction. It will be seen that the rosettes are attached to each of its sides, thereby increasing the thickness of the plank which receives the stalactends and a facing rosette, as may be seen in the front view A. The side of the console is fluted to a proper marginal distance from the rosette.

Fig. 8 will need no explanation, its construction being very similar to Fig. 1.

Fig. 2 represents a console of a different character. The sides or flanks, embracing the semi-honeysuckle, are made of inch boards, between which is a thick plank, to which the sides are attached. The face of this centre plank is sculptured as represented in the figure; or it may consist of only a plain, sunken panel. The pyramidal circles in the sides are turned in a lathe, and made fast by means of screws. The small semicircle, or footing, is also turned and joined to the console, as the design shows.

The other figures on this Plate need no explanation, as they are very plain, and may be measured in any of their details from the annexed scale.

PLATE XXI.

On this Plate are fragments of designs, sections, and plans for inside finish. Fig. 1 shows an elevation of a parlor finish for windows and doors. A plan of the face casing, jamb, and door stile, may be seen at **A**. **D** represents a section of the cornice, thickness of casing, and console. The rosette or corner block should be of equal thickness with the face casing. The dotted lines on Fig. 1 show the joint for the casing and block, which should be dressed flush and smooth. The inner edge of the face casing, which rounds down to the jamb, should mitre at the angle. It will then be seen that the square of the block must be just equal to the face of the casing, not, however, including the inner moulding, to be mitred as above mentioned. The face casing can be fluted with the common round, nearly to the end, the circles of which can be finished out with the gouge.

Every part of this design was drawn, and should be measured, with the scale of feet and inches **R**, as, also, all the parts of Figs. 2, 3, and 4.

Fig. 2 is the elevation of another window and door, their finish having the same profile of face casing as will be seen in plan **B**. The construction of the cap and break, in Fig. 2, will be sufficiently well understood by the figures. The arch of the corner may be

PLATE XXI.   87

turned in a lathe, and then cut into four quarter circles, the fluting in the face casing made to meet and correspond with the flutes in the corner blocks, and made to continue flush and smooth as one piece.

In Fig. 3 is an elevation of a cheap, but neat, design for a window and door finish. A plan of the face casing and cap is seen directly below the figure. It will be needless to give any farther explanations of the design. C, H, and N, represent three designs for base by sections. These several designs for base were drawn by scale O and should be measured by the same.

Fig. 5 shows a plan of sliding doors, in which it is only necessary to extend a railway into the opening from the hollow wall the width of a single door on each side, as it will be seen that each of the two middle doors swings back against the one to which it is attached, and slides into the partition double. This figure needs no further explanation, except to remark that the span of the room is divided into six equal parts, two of which are for the reception of the sliding doors, and four for the opening for the doors.

Fig. 4 is a semi-plan of Fig. 5 enlarged, showing the door stiles and panels, in which it will be perceived that the stile first entering the partition has a sufficient width to receive a stop attached with glue or screws to the side, thereby closing the opening, and yet exhibiting the common width of the other stiles. W, in Fig. 4, is the railway and hollow wall.

PLATE XXII.

On this Plate is a design for a small but very convenient Cottage; indeed, combining nearly, if not quite, as many domestic conveniences as the amount of room and cost of construction can afford; and yet it exhibits a neat and tasteful exterior.

The main part is 16 by 32, on the plan, and 15 feet high. The wing is 15 by 16 feet, on the plan, and 13 feet high.

The bed-room, bath-room, and nursery, are under the roof of the veranda, as may be seen in the elevation, and also by the ground and chamber plans.

The walls of this house may be constructed according to the design on Plate XXIII, Fig. 3; but it would be better if built in the manner of Fig. 5, Plate XXIV, which is probably the best mode of construction for a house of this kind.

The gable cornice may be embellished with a fringe; or it may be plain, as is represented in the elevation.

The elevation represents the style of windows, chimneys, and veranda or porch.

The inside finish is unimportant, except that it should be of the general character and style of the outside.

PLATE XVIII.   89

PLATE XXIII.

Fig. 1 represents an elevation of a frame, to be covered with perpendicular boards and battens, where, it will be seen, studs are necessary on each side of the doors and windows. In each of the piers, as well as over and under the windows, are horizontal ribs, to which the perpendicular boards are to be nailed.

The window and door studs should be one inch wider than the ribs; and then nail perpendicular pieces to the ribs on the inside, as seen at *t t t t.*

g g g, Fig. 3, are the ribs, and *k k* the window studs. *x x* are the sills, P P the joists, *h h h h h* the battens, and *y* the corner post, the inner corner of which is rabbetted to receive the lath on the same line with the studs and furring. Fig. 3 was drawn, and should be measured by the subjoined scale.

Fig. 2 shows a method of framing a rafter, *p* being the rafter, and *g* a section of the plate.

Fig. 4 represents an end elevation of a frame for the design on Plate XXV. It is to be covered with common siding. Farther explanation is not needed.

PLATE XXIV.

Fig. 1, on this Plate, shows the manner of constructing the frame for the design on Plate XXII.

Fig. 5 is an enlarged horizontal section or plan of Fig. 1. *g*, Fig. 5, shows the sill; *h h h h h*, the plank, the outside of which should be dressed; *x x x x x*, the battens and corner boards; P P P P P P, sections of the small studs or furrings, used to strengthen the joints of the plank, to which the planks are nailed, and also to receive the lath on the inside.

Fig. 8 is a design for an outside finish for windows.

Fig. 7 shows a section of the cornice and a profile of the bracket for Fig. 8.

Fig. 6 presents a fragment of the porch for the design on Plate XXII. D, Fig. 6, is the column; V, the lintel; and C, the bracket.

Fig. D shows the manner of fitting the bracket to the column and lintel.

Fig. 2 represents an elevation of a pendant and gable cornice, together with two designs for ornamenting the arris of the barge and roof. The figures in either of the designs on the crown mould of Fig. 2, should be made of two-inch plank. The designs *k k k k* are separate pieces attached to the crown mould at regular intervals. But the design in Z Z is one continued plank.

Fig. 4 shows the pinnacle for the pendant for Fig. 2.

Fig. 3 is a horizontal section of the base of the spire to the pinnacle.

PLATE XXV.   91

The accompanying scale will measure all the figures on this Plate, with the exception of Fig. 1.

PLATE XXV.

On this Plate is a design for a Cottage of the bracketed style, the walls of which are to be covered with common siding. An end elevation is represented on Plate XXIII, Fig. 4.

The arrangements of the several apartments of this design are clearly defined on the ground and chamber plans, to which is annexed a scale of feet and inches by which to measure their several parts. The elevation on Plate XXV was drawn from a scale of double the size of the one here annexed.

It will be seen by the chamber plan, that the vestibule tower extends into the chamber sufficient to make four equal sides to its plan. The room on the chamber plan within the tower, is designed for a library. This tower is carried up through the roof sufficiently high to clear the cornice and brackets on the back side of the tower from the roof of the main part, as may be seen in the frame, Fig. 4, Plate XXIII.

The style of the bracket for the cornice may be found on Plate XX, where there is a sufficient variety from which to select a design. The style of windows is given in the elevation.

The balcony seen in the elevation is partly of iron, yet may be constructed entirely of wood.

A style of finish for the parlor may be found on Plate II, Fig. 4; and a finish for a dining room on Plate IV, Fig. 1.

PLATE XXVI.

This Plate comprises thirteen designs, in outline sketches, for country and village residences, each varying from the others in form of outline, as well as in its interior arrangement. These several sketches are offered to the student as bases in designing. The variety of exterior and internal construction being presented on a single Plate will afford an opportunity to compare each design with the others, and enable the student to select one suited to his wants, without a search through an entire volume.

The design in Fig. 1 should be finished in the Rural Gothic style. The main body of the house, as will be seen in the plan, is in the form of a T. That portion of the building containing the wood-house and pantry is but one story, and is covered with a shed roof. A veranda is continued from the entrance at one end of the hall around the parlor to the entrance into the other. It will be seen in the plan, that the hall is back of the parlor, the stairs ascending from it to the chamber.

The veranda may be a deck-roof, a sash-door opening out upon it from the front gable.

Fig. 2 is a two-story cottage, with a hip-roof, and is to be finished with consoles or brackets. The entrance to the hall is on the side, instead of the front. A veranda may be constructed on the front of the house, and continued round the angle to the entrance. This design is suitable for a residence in country or town.

PLATE XXVI.   93

Fig. 3 should be finished in the bracketed style. A balcony is designed for the second story, in the vestibule. The stairs should ascend from the left side of the vestibule.

Fig. 4 is a cottage of but one story, the parlor situated nearly in the centre, with a hall continuing from the entrance in the front porch to the rear of the house, and also to the dining room, which is situated at the right of the parlor. The plan will show that nearly every room in the house may be entered from the hall.

The ceiling of the parlor is in the roof of the cupola, and is lighted with stained glass above the roof of the main body, and by two windows below, descending to the floor, and opening from the porch in front.

The kitchen is situated in the rear of the dining room. A veranda is attached to it, 5 by 20 feet. The nursery is in front of the dining room.

The cornice, in this design, should be decorated with rich and heavy consoles, arranged in pairs, in both the main and cupola cornices.

Fig. 5 presents a plan of a residence differing in decoration from those preceding. As is seen in the elevation, the vestibule tower consists of three stories, the stairs ascending to the third story.

The parlor is 18 by 21 feet, on the plan, and the ceiling 15 feet above the floor. The dining room is 17 by 20 feet, on the plan, and 9 feet to the ceiling, which is the height of all the rooms on the first floor, with the exception of the parlor.

The cook-room is 13 by 13 feet; the nursery, 11 by 14; and the library, 14 by 17.

A veranda at the entrance of the side of the vestibule, extends along the front of the library.

That portion of the building comprising the library and dining room, is two stories in height; that containing the kitchen and nursery, one and a half stories, covered with a shed-roof; and that containing the bed-room, back of the kitchen, 8 by 10 feet, and the pantry, 8 by 8 feet, is of one story, also covered with a shed-roof.

This design should be finished in the bracketed style; and balconies should be constructed in the second and third stories of the tower.

Fig. 6 is a design in the Grecian style, with a colonade front, and with attic windows in the frieze.

Fig. 7 is a plan of a small house, with a one-story vestibule at the entrance, having a concave roof. The upright part comprises the parlor and dining room, with the hall passing between them to the kitchen in the rear.

The nursery is 9 by 11 feet, and is entered from the dining room.

The part comprising the kitchen, nursery, and pantry, is but one story high. It has a shed and hip-roof. The form of the roof in the upright part, may be seen in the elevation.

The decorations to this cottage should be in the Rural Gothic style.

Fig. 8. The ground plan and elevation, in this design, is sufficiently clear to explain itself. It is to be finished in the Rural Gothic style.

Fig. 9. The construction of this design is very simple. The Grecian, or bracket style, may be employed upon it.

Fig. 10. This design is the smallest and cheapest on the Plate, yet is convenient for a small family. It may be finished in the Rural Gothic, or in the Grecian style of architecture. Constructing a

PLATE XXVI.   95

veranda in the front of the wing, would add much to the beauty and convenience of the house.

Fig. 11. The form and construction of this design may be understood from the Figure. It should be finished in the Rural Gothic style.

Fig. 12 differs much from the others, yet may be understood from the plan and elevation. It will be seen that the span of the roof, on the main part, extends from the front to the rear, and should, therefore, be finished in the bracketed style.

Fig. 13. The upright part, in this design, embraces only the hall, parlor, dining room, and stairs. The portion of the building containing the kitchen and nursery is of but one story, with a concave roof, as may be seen in the elevation of a part of the kitchen. A small veranda is in front of the kitchen, the roof of which joins the roof of the kitchen in the hip-angle. There is also a veranda in front of the main part, the roof of which may be constructed with or without a balcony.

The communication to the cellar is through the narrow passage between the stairs and the kitchen. The communication to the chamber is by stairs ascending from the hall between partitions or walls.

This house should be finished in the bracketed style.

All the figures on this Plate were drawn from the accompanying scale. It will be noted, that the small divisions at the left end of the scale represent feet, and the larger divisions each ten feet.

PLATE XXVII.

On this Plate are five designs for gable fringes, or ornamented barge-boards, in connection with their respective crown moulds and pendants.

The several designs here given should be worked in plank that is two inches in thickness. Fig. 1 is the pinnacle to the pendant in Fig. 5, seen at the foot of the barge, to form the angle with the eaves. Fig. 7 is the stalactend to the same pendant. The position of this pendant in relation to the cornice and wall, can be seen in the Figure U J, U being a horizontal section of the shaft of the pinnacle, and J a section of the corner or angle of the wall. The dotted line g determines the projection of the eave cornice from the wall J; and the dotted line y designates the projection of the raking cornice from the wall J.

It is only necessary to add, that all the figures on this Plate were drawn from the subjoined scale, and should, of course, be measured by the same.

PLATE XXVIII. 97

PLATE XXVIII.

On Plate **XXVIII** are two designs for inside window casing, **and** also two designs for base.

Fig. 1 represents a window elevation, with two compartments, paneled below the sash frames.

Fig. 3 shows a horizontal section, or plan, of Fig. 1.

Fig. 5 shows an enlarged plan of Fig. 1. *w* Is the jamb; *n*, the face casing; *y y*, the sash stiles; *u*, parting stops; *r*, inside stops; and *o*, the band moulding, which is joined to the base by a quarter circle, and may be seen in Fig. 1. **J** represents a section of the base, on top of which is the moulding which is continued around the outer edge of the door and window casing.

Fig. 2 shows an elevation of a window or door casing for a house of peculiar construction. It is, therefore, necessary, first, to notice the construction of the house before entering upon a description of the window casing. This casing is designed to be employed on a house, the outer walls of which are boards, dressed on both sides and matched. The frame, or timbers, supporting the floor, joists, or ceiling, to be of scantling, 4 by 4 inches, to which timbers the boards are nailed. The joists are to be placed on top of the scantling, and the ceiling to be plastered; or, the joists may be 3 by 7, and dressed, in which case, the outside timbers should be also 3 by 7. The edges of the joists should be flush with the edges of the timbers. Then dress both sides of the floor boards, as the joists and floor will constitute the ceiling. The plate will be also of scantling, and supported by nails through the upper ends of the perpendicular boards which constitute the outside wall.

It will be seen that, in this building, posts, studs, braces, and even lath and plaster on the walls, are entirely dispensed with. But, to give greater security to the joist timbers, the peculiar window casing, as seen in Fig. 2, has been designed.

Fig. 4 shows the plan of the window casing and sash, and also a fragment of the siding with the outside battens.

Fig. 6 represents an enlarged plan of one side of Fig. 4. *x* Shows a plan of the jamb and face casing, made of a solid scantling; *g* shows a piece of the siding; *b*, outside casing; *o o*, sash; *u*, parting stops; *o r*, inside stops. The upright scantling *x* is of sufficient length to support the joist timbers in the ceiling or floor.

The scale below Figs. 1 and 2 will measure any part of Figs. 1, 2, 3, and 4; and the scale on the right hand of the plate will measure any part of Figs. 5 and 6, and also the designs for base, J and F.

A small house may be constructed in this manner, at a very trifling expense, as it may be nearly or quite enclosed at the cost of an ordinary frame; and when enclosed, its inside finish is nearly complete. A house of this kind can be made as comfortable and dry as one clapboarded and with inside walls of lath and plaster, and with a little embellishment on the cornice, makes a neat and tasty appearance.

PLATES XXIX, XXX.

These Plates illustrate the first principles in linear perspective; and it will be necessary for the student, in studying this diagram, to be exceedingly careful in tracing each line to its proper termination according to its reference.

Let the rectangular figure in the diagram, in Fig. 1, be the plan of the cube of which to erect a perpendicular view as it would appear to the eye from the point of sight A. First, draw the line A P; then draw the line A B (Fig. 1,) and A D (Fig. 1;) then draw the line F P H (Fig. 1,) at right angle with the line A P. Then the line F P H is called the perspective plane.

Perpendicular to A B and A D (Fig. 1,) draw the lines B C and D E (Fig. 1,) and make B C and D E (Fig. 1,) equal to the elevation of the cube above the eye. Then from C and E (Fig. 1,) produce the lines C A and E A. From A D, at F, and A B, at H, (Fig. 1,) erect the perpendiculars F C and H I.

Draw the line J R (Fig. 2,) at right angle to the line A P (Fig. 1,) and at a sufficient distance below the plan to erect the view of the cube. Then draw the lines F F G and H H I parallel to A P. Take the distance B C or D E (Fig. 1,) which is the elevation of the cube above the eye, and set it from C to B (Fig. 2;) then take the distance H I (Fig. 1,) and make I H in Fig. 2. Then with the distance F C (Fig. 1,) make G F (Fig. 2.) Join F B, (Fig. 2,) and produce the line to **J**, as a vanishing point on the line of the horizon **J R**. Produce the line **B H** (Fig. 2,) until it touches the horizon line **J R**, for the other vanishing point.

The student will here perceive that the horizon line and the line **B H** will not meet unless they are both produced to an inconvenient distance. To obviate this difficulty, the instrument denominated the "concentograph," is used in drawing the converging lines in perspective. This instrument is represented in connection with the horizon line in Fig. 2. It will be noticed, that the angle of the legs of this instrument may be changed by turning the nuts on the centre screw, in the hollow square of the shank. By this operation, the angle can be made much sharper than is represented in the diagram; or, the legs may be made to produce a continued straight line from the extremity of one leg to that of the other.

In setting the concentograph, the following directions should be carefully observed:

First, place the edge of the blade **G C I K** on the line **B H**, and, with a pencil against the outside of the legs, make the lines 3 4 and 3 2; then on the line of 3 4, and at one-third or one-fourth the distance, drive the pin seen at **N**; then slide the instrument down, keeping the leg against the pin, and place the edge of the blade on the horizon line **J R**. Draw the line 1 5, by the edge of the blade, and where it crosses the line 3 2, drive another pin. Now, by keeping the legs of the instrument against the pins, and moving it to any other point, the line drawn by the edge **G C I K** will tend to the vanishing point, or to the point where the line **B H** would meet the horizon line **J R**.

The instrument is now set, and all lines tending to the vanishing point will be drawn by it. The first line to find is the bottom o base of the cube. Take such a distance as is presumed to be equal to the elevation of the eye above the bottom of the cube, and set it from C to X, Fig. 2, and V H B X will be one of the sides of the cube. Then at J, the other vanishing point, drive a pin, against which place a rule of sufficient length to draw X J, and W X B F will be the other side of the cube, as seen from the point of sight A; and all lines tending to this vanishing point will be drawn by the rule against the pin at J.

Let us now suppose this cube to be the body of a house, in which we wish to represent windows and doors. On the rectangular plan of the given cube, designate the figure of each opening for the proposed windows and doors, and of each feature of the house to be represented in the perspective view. Then from each point of angle formed by the several features of the building, as exhibited on Plate XXX, Fig. 1, draw lines in the direction of the point of sight A, touching the perspective plane F P H; and from the point at which these converging lines touch the perspective plane, draw perpendicular lines, as on Fig. 2, Plate XXX. It will now be seen that lines drawn to the plane in the direction of the point of sight, as above described, and thence to Fig. 2, that the width of each opening, its position and depth of jamb, are represented precisely as they would appear to the eye from the point of sight A.

To determine the lines for the tops and bottoms of the windows, lay off the proper distances, according to the scale of the plan, Fig. 1. On the perpendicular line C B, Fig. 2, and from these points on C B, with the instrument working on the pins as before directed, designate the tops and bottoms of the windows, as seen by the dotted lines, Fig. 2.

The same process should be followed in representing each of

the several features of the building, the sides of which fall within the vision from the point of sight **A.**

To erect the roof, set up from **B,** on the line **A B P,** the elevation of the ridge above the line of the eaves, at 3, Fig. 1, and, with the instrument on **J,** draw from 3 to 4, which is the line drawn from the plan of the point of the gable; and, with the same instrument, determine the rear cornice projection. Then join **B** 4 and **F** 4 for the raking line of the gable.

The student will readily perceive that this rule, when rightly applied, will represent any and all objects presented from the same point of view; and a close examination of Plate **XXX** will enable him to comprehend and apply it in the different positions of a building without farther explanation.

PLATE XXXI.

On this Plate is a design for a Cottage, in the **Rural Gothic** style. It will be seen, on the ground plan, that the entrance to the vestibule is on the side, and that the parlor is entered under the stairs.

In this design it will be well to extend the veranda around the sitting-room until it joins the vestibule at the entrance. This veranda should have a deck roof, surrounded with a balustrade. It will add much to the appearance of the house, and furnish a very pleasant and airy balcony, as well as an elegant and convenient veranda.

The elevation was drawn from a scale twice as large as the one accompanying the ground and chamber plans, so that an inch on the scale is but half an inch when applied to the elevation.

The manner of constructing the frame is in accordance with the

PLATE XXXI.   103

illustrations given on Plate XXIII, Fig. 1 and Fig. 2, where the adjustment of the window studs, ribs, siding, and battens, are clearly defined.

External Finish.—The eave cornice, on this cottage, may be constructed after the design given on Plate X, Fig. 1, where the raking cornice is illustrated in connection with the fringe. A section of the eave cornice may be seen on Plate X, Fig. 6. The fringe for the vestibule gable may also be seen on Plate X, Fig. 1. For other gable fringes there is a sufficient number of examples in this work from which to select the several designs, and the effect would be better to select a different design of fringe for the several gables on this form of cottage. But the crown mould and facia should be continued round the entire building, the rakes included.

The windows may be finished as seen in the perspective view; or other examples may be selected, but of such a character as would correspond with the style of the house. It would be well to construct a portion of them with two compartments, and I would recommend one bay window for the parlor. Designs for pendants in the gables should be selected of various forms.

Inside Finish.—A design for the parlor casing may be found on Plate XXI, Fig. 2; and one for the sitting-room may be made out of the same, by omitting the break in the top casing; but, in other respects, not differing from the parlor finish. The casing for the dining room should be comparatively plain. Appropriate designs might be selected from Fig. 3, Plate XXI. For the rest of the inside finish, the builder can select such a design as he may deem proper for each respective room.

This residence is designed to be located on a corner lot, that it may front on two streets, yet it would answer on a single street.

PLATE XXXII.

Fig. 1 in the Plate, is an elevation of a bay window. The sash, in the window, is designed to slide, in the manner of the common window. Fig. 2 is a plan of the window, and Fig. 3 represents a section of the cornice. Further explanation of the construction of this window is unnecessary, as the subjoined scale will measure any part of all the figures on this plate.

Fig. 4 is the elevation of a pendant, designed for the Rural Gothic style of building.

A plan, or horizontal section, is seen in Fig. 6.

In the construction of this pendant, it will be necessary, first, to shape a board like Fig. 5. The grooves should be sunk in the sides of the board before the edges are formed. The object of the grooves is, to receive the boards which form the angles. These boards, which are of half width, will of course have the same form of outward edge as the wide board first cut. They should be glued into the grooves, and when the three pieces are united, the horizontal section will be in the form of a cross, as seen in **R R.** Boards are then cut to fit the angles at the dotted lines in Fig. 5, and made to form a square, as seen in the section **Y Y.** **K K,** Fig. 6, are triangular pieces fitted into the flanks of the shaft, running from the stalactend to the pinnacle.

R, Fig. 6, is a small square member reaching from the stalactend to the raking cornice or barge-board. The small triangles in Fig. 4, are made by cutting notches into the projecting corner of this square member. The small figure in the angle of the pinnacle, may be first turned in a lathe, and then carved and cut into quarters, and placed into the four angles of the pinnacle.

A pendant constructed in this way may be cheaply and quickly executed. One advantage of this mode of construction is, that if we retain a pattern of the board, Fig. 5, we can construct other pendants with new and different ornaments in the angles, thereby changing the features of the whole design.

PLATE XXXIII, XXXIV.

On Plate **XXXIII** are the ground and chamber plans for a small Cottage, a perspective view of which is seen on Plate **XXXIV**. It will be observed, that this design is very conveniently arranged, in both the first and second stories, especially if we take into consideration the space it occupies and the cost of its construction. It is **32** by **24** feet, on the plan, and **15** feet high. The vestibule is **4** by **9**, on the plan, and of the same height of the main body.

The arrangement and size of the several apartments are made sufficiently plain and intelligible by the plans, to need no further description.

This cottage may be constructed of stone, brick, or wood. If built of stone, the size of the plan should be increased sufficiently to give to the several apartments the dimensions designated in the plan, as the arrangements as here seen were made for a wood structure.

External Finish.—The cornice designed for this cottage may be found in detail on Plate IX, clearly illustrated and explained. We may, however, with propriety, employ a different style of fringe. On Plate IX are also a plan and elevation for the chimney and top.

The style of the windows are seen in the perspective view. The frieze should be 12 inches wide under the eave cornice. The covering of the walls may consist of common siding, perpendicular boards, or plank, as circumstances or taste may dictate.

Internal Finish.—The builder may select such a style of inside finish, for the several apartments, as may best conform to his taste and the circumstances of the case.

PLATE XXXV.

On this Plate are three designs for verandas, and one for a balcony supported with brackets.

Fig. 1 represents a fragment of a design for a veranda. The arch in this design is made in two separate pieces of two-inch plank, and joins in the centre of the arch, with the foot resting on the capital of the column.

Fig. 2 is a section of the cornice.

Fig. 5 shows a plan of the column. This column may be made of boards mitred at the angles; or it may be solid, as seen in the plan, Fig. 5.

Fig. 4 is a design for a veranda of similar character of Fig. 1, but differing in detail. The balustrade is made of two-inch plank, framed into the pillars two inches above the roof. In the architrave

PLATE XXXV.   **107**

are niches cut through an inch board, back of which a lining is fixed to close the apertures. The arches in this design should be made of two-inch plank, and joined in the centre as in Fig. 1.

Fig. 7 shows the plan of the column seen in Fig. 4.

Fig. 3 is an elevation of another veranda of nearly the same character, but differing in the details of its construction. A section of the cornice and lintel may be seen in Fig. 11; D D representing the rafter; I I, the ribs or beams for the roof boards; A, the roof boards; G, the crown mould; N, modillion; E, the furring to which the frieze is nailed; and R, the lintel.

Fig. 10 shows the plan of the column. The roof, in either of these designs, may be constructed of matched boards, nearly level, and covered with zinc. Tin is not as good.

Fig. 8 represents a roof of boards and battens, yet the same may be decked and surrounded with a balustrade, thus converting it into a balcony. A profile of the brackets employed by pairs may be seen in the return cornice in Fig. 8.

Fig. 9 represents a fragment of a design for a balcony. The drapery under the floor is cut out of an inch board. The supporting bracket is seen in Fig. 3. This bracket, and, indeed, all brackets made of wood for the support of balconies, should be made of two or three-inch oak plank, as far as the first bearing of the floor.

Fig. 6 shows a section of the panel. D is the top rail; E, the bottom rail.

The subjoined scale measures any part of all the figures on this Plate.

PLATE XXXVI.

Fig. 2, on this Plate, represents a fragment of a design for a light wood veranda.   Fig. 4 is a horizontal section of the corner or angular column, and Fig. 5 is a horizontal section of one of the intermediate columns.   Fig. 3 is a section of the roof boards, plate, frieze, and cornice; R, Fig. 3, being the cornice seen at R, Fig. 2. S is the plate into which the rafter is sunk, by a gain, as seen by the dotted lines G, the plate S being of sufficient width to receive the entire depth of the rafters.   E, Fig. 3, is the open frieze, seen in Fig. 2, at E.   The columns reach to the plate S, in Fig. 2, and the open frieze, E is cut between the columns.

In this veranda, it is designed to have the rafters made of one inch-and-a-half plank, neatly dressed, as the roof will constitute the ceiling.   Ribs should be placed between the rafters, of the same thickness and depth of the rafters.   The rafters may be 3 feet apart, but these ribs not more than 16 inches.   One of them should be nailed to the ends of the rafters, as seen in Fig. 3, by the dark section at the end of the rafter.   The next bearer, which serves as a rib, is the plate at G.

The roof should be covered with boards five-eighths of an inch thick, perfectly sound, well-seasoned, and planed on both the upper and under sides, the joints battened with lumber of a similar kind. The roof boards must have small grooves on the upper sides, near the edges of the boards, that the battens will cover, in order that the

PLATE XXXVI.   109

water which is driven under the battens may pass off in these chan-
nels at the eaves.

The curve and length of the rafters can be found by the curve
seen in the roof, in Fig. 2. The subjoined scale will measure all the
figures on the Plate.

A veranda of this character makes the best appearance with just
four columns. There may, however, be *more* than four, but it is
difficult to get along with less. Two would be better than three.
If the space is too limited to admit of four columns of equal spaces,
it would be well to make a wide space in the middle, the outer
spaces much less. Columns adjusted in this manner are in nearly
as good taste as if they stood equidistant. However, the spaces
between the columns should be made equal, unless the veranda is
less than 15 feet long.

Should the builder find some of the designs for open columns
in Plate XIII better conforming to his taste than the one above
described, he should not hesitate to select from them; yet he should
not forget that it would be much preferable to employ a figure in the
frieze differing from the one used in the columns.

A better, though more expensive, roof for a veranda, may be
understood by observing the following directions: Let the rafters
have a slower curve than is represented in Fig. 2. Dress them
neatly, as before directed. Place them nearer together than is
necessary for a roof constructed of boards and battens—not more
than 18 or 20 inches apart—in which case ribs will not be necessary,
except the one at the ends of the rafters and the plate, seen at G,
Fig. 3. Dress and match some narrow boards for the roof, mitring
them on the hip rafters and placing the smooth side down, which
will constitute the ceiling. Over these boards put on a covering of

the common roof boards to receive the shingles. Shingles of a uniform width—about six inches—should be selected, the butt ends of which should be carved into the shape of the small end of an egg, letting the curve on each edge of the shingle extend up as far as the shingle is laid to the weather—say, three and a half or four inches. It may be necessary to add, however, that the *first course* should be laid with square ends, after which, the entire roof should be covered with shingles of oval formed ends, as above described, placing their points directly over the joints in the preceding course, somewhat resembling the scales on a fish. A roof of this kind is perfect proof against water, and is showy and durable.

Fig. 6, Plate **XXXVI**, shows an elevation, or front view, of a balcony. Fig. 1 is an outside view of Fig. 6 below the floor and balustrade. **K** shows the timber on which the floor rests; **R**, the lower part of the pendant; and **N** the supporting bracket.

The lower rail in the balustrade should be placed one and one-half inches above the floor. The arches on the balustrade are constructed of inch boards by cutting the several figures into forms somewhat resembling the letter **Y**. But it should be observed, that, in constructing these arches, the grains in the wood should be perpendicular. These several figures should be attached to the panel boards by means of screws, and found at the point of the arch, being first beveled on the inner edge, as seen in Fig. 6.

The small figures within the arches are openings cut through an inch board, to which the arches are attached. Farther explanation is unnecessary, as the scale will determine the dimensions of the several parts in this design; and also measure all the details of the Plate.

In the construction of balconies, the builder may suit his own

PLATE XXXVII.   111

taste in selecting designs for balustrades, pendants, and brackets, the object of this design being merely to afford an easy and simple method of constructing this convenient and, we may say, almost indispensable appendage to a dwelling.

Balconies are frequently constructed of iron, of various designs, which may be obtained at foundries in most of our large towns, and at trifling expense. Their light and airy construction makes a very beautiful appearance, as it seems expressive of the purpose for which they were designed.

PLATE XXXVII.

A design is here represented for a Farm-house.

It will be noticed, by the ground plan and elevation, that the vestibule consists of but a single story, and that a roof is constructed over the entrance, supported by brackets, the projection of which should be at least 3 feet, the platform below being made to conform in width.

External Finish.—A suitable design for a bracket may be found on Plate XX, Fig. 5. The projection of the bracket will determine the projection of the roof. The brackets should be arranged before shingling. The first roof board should be dressed on the under side to constitute the planceer. This board should be one and one quarter inches thick, or the nails may pass through the planceer. A crown moulding should be nailed to the edge of the planceer, and extend down on the bracket 2 inches, upon which the shingles will rest, thus completing the cornice. The bracket, however, as seen in the elevation, is constructed differently, and is much less expensive. As there exhibited, it consists in merely framing the rafter to project over the plate, cutting the end perpendicular. The part of the rafter extending below the plate must be dressed. The planceer and crown mould are as above described. The roof board, or planceer to the rake, should be placed parallel with the rake, under which must be placed blocks of the same depth, thickness, and projection, of those in the eave cornice, their ends resting against the frieze. The frieze may be from 10 to 16 inches below the eave, and of sufficient width on the rake to intersect with the one under the eave. The cornice on the vestibule is of the same character, but of less projection. The style of window frames may be seen in the elevation.

Internal Finish.— The arrangement of the several apartments of the interior explain themselves sufficiently in the plan. The style of casing is left to the choice of the builder.

The ground plan and elevation, on this Plate, were drawn from the accompanying scale. The small divisions on the scale represent feet, and the larger ones are each five feet in space.

PLATE XXXVIII.

On this Plate is a design for a two-story Cottage in the bracketed style. It is to be of wood, the walls covered with boards, either in a horizontal or perpendicular position. It will be seen by the ground plan that the parlor and drawing-room extend out from the flanks of the walls of the main body, and are only one story in height.

PLATE XXXVIII. **113**

By reason of this projection of a part of the walls it would be difficult to support a brick or stone wall, in the second story, over such projection, and hence the necessity of walls of wood. Even if built of wood, it will be necessary to frame a truss at this point, to prevent the plastering from cracking in the ceiling of the parlor and drawing-room.

It should be observed, that the cornice of the main body of the building is in a straight, unbroken line, yet the front wall is recessed back to the vestibule, both in the first and second stories. This will give a roof to the balcony in the second story, and admit light to the second story of the vestibule, by means of a sash door opening out upon the roof of the veranda.

The walls of the recess in the second story, are on the same plan with those of the first, as seen in the elevation and plan.

The vestibule is an octagon on its plan, and has three stories, with circular stairs ascending from the first to the third story.

External Finish.—The projection of the cornice should be supported by consoles similar to Fig. 1, or Fig. 8, on Plate XX, and the planceer should be horizontal and not parallel with the plane of the roof, as in the bracketed style constructed with gables. The projection of the roof may be determined by the bracket or console.

A very suitable design for a veranda for this cottage may be found in Fig. 1 of Plate XXXV, or in Fig. 4 on the same Plate.

The style of window casing is seen in the elevation. The front windows of the parlor and drawing-room have three compartments.

Inside Finish.—The communication between the vestibule, parlor, and drawing-room, is by double doors, made to swing into the corners or angles of the several rooms.

A good parlor finish will be found in Fig. 2, Plate XXI; and a drawing-room finish in Fig. 1 of the same Plate. For a design for the casing in the dining room, I would refer the builder to Plate XI, Fig. 1; and for the family room, to 3 on the same Plate.

PLATES XXXIX, XL.

In this publication the author has thought he could best serve the interests of the builder by treating only on such branches of the science of building as were within his constant field of labor. The construction of private residences is a department of the science in which the country builder is mostly engaged, while churches and other public edifices are generally designed by experienced architects. Thus it has been thought advisable, in this treatise, not to introduce the subject of ornamental finish for expensive public buildings. Yet, for the gratification of the few who may feel an interest in the subject of church building, a design is presented, on Plates XXXIX and XL, for a church edifice suitable for a large country town.

This design is so simple in its arrangements that builders of but moderate skill and experience may safely undertake its construction. The walls, including the columns, are built of rubble stone. The pinnacles, window-caps, and window sills, should be of cut stone or cast iron. If iron, they should be painted in imitation of stone. The drapery in the steeple should be of cast iron.

Plate XXXIX exhibits a plan of the basement and also of the principal floor, from which it will be seen that the orchestre is situated within the tower and over the vestibule. At each end of the vestibule is an open staircase ascending to the principal floor. At the landing of the main stairs are stairs for ascending to the orchestre, which is elevated only five feet above the principal floor, and is immediately back of the pulpit. In case of the construction of a gallery, stairs should ascend from the landing of the orchestre stairs, on a quarter circle, over the main stairs, to a landing on a level with the gallery. From this landing commence the stairs ascending into the tower.

The entrance to the basement is directly opposite to the entrance into the vestibule.

The windows in the flanks of the edifice may have horizontal heads with hood caps; or they may be slightly arched with rubble stone, thus saving the expense of caps. The latter mode might be recommended as a matter of economy, and the same kind of caps may be employed in the circular heads to the windows in the front of the edifice. If the windows in the flanks have *horizontal* heads, their caps should be similar to those seen in the elevation for the basement or of the vestibule. If they are *arched*, they should rise in the centre of the arch 10 inches, the arch being turned with rubble stone fair with the common face of the wall.

The spire should be constructed of wood, and covered with shingles, the lower ends of which being shaped like the scales of a fish, and then sanded in paint, in imitation of stone.

The entire tower, below the spire, should be of rubble stone, though the two upper sections *might* be built of wood, if thought advisable as a matter of economy. If the walls of the tower are constructed of stone, it will be necessary to change the rectangular or square form of the tower, which rises out of the roof, into one of the octagonal form for the belfry. To accomplish this, it will be necessary to place four strong wood lintels across the corner of the square section rising out of the roof. These timbers should be placed in the walls of the tower below the roof, to form the angles and foundation for the octagon walls. Over these lintels strong arches should be turned, to resist the pressure of the walls on the lintels.

The windows in the flanks of the house should be placed two feet above the principal floor, and extend up to within three feet of the ceiling. The basement windows should be similar in construction to those seen in the basement of the elevation. The ceiling in the body of the building should be arched, the arch extending two feet down the walls and three on the ceiling, both edges of the arch terminating with a stucco moulding.

Any farther description of this design is unnecessary, as the length and breadth of the edifice, as well as the size of the several apartments, are plainly figured on the plans, accompanying which is also a scale with which all the details of both plates may be measured.

PLATE .XLI.

This Plate exhibits a design for a Cottage in the Rural Gothic style. The arrangement of the several apartments, or general design of the building, is represented in the plan.

The perspective view shows the form of the roof, style of windows, position of the chimneys, and entrance to the vestibule.

PLATE XLII. **117**

It should be observed, however, that all of the plan that is in the rear of the dining room and family room will be the height of only one story, with a shed roof.

External Finish.—A suitable design for a veranda may be found on Plate XXXVI, Fig. 2, yet there are others that would answer equally as well.

A design for the gable cornice on the parlor front may be found in Fig. 1, Plate X.   A suitable pendant for this gable may be seen in Fig. 4, Plate XXXII.

A fringe for the small gable over the veranda may be seen in Fig. 4, Plate XXVII.

A fringe for the dining room gable with a suitable pendant, may be found in Fig. 2, Plate X.

It should be observed, that the cornice mouldings for the eaves are to be carried up the rakes.

Inside Finish.—In selecting designs for the interior finish of the several apartments, the builder should give a proper variety, discriminating according to the character and purpose of each respective room.

PLATE XLII.

ARCHITECTURAL MOULDINGS.

The various combinations of mouldings are made up by the following list:

A, Plate XLII, representing the torus, mostly employed in the Grecian and Roman columns.

B, the astragal, employed in different places, and in most of the various combinations of mouldings.

C, the echinus. It is employed in the capitals of some of the Grecian and Roman columns, and in various other places.

D, the ovalo. It is used in place of the echinus, but differs from it by its curve being part of an ellipse, while that of the echinus is part of a circle.

E, the scotia, mostly used in the base of columns.

F, the cavetto or cove, used in most combinations of mouldings.

G, the cymatium, frequently employed in cornices and in many other situations.

H, the cymareversara, or ogee, variously employed with other mouldings.

I, the fillet, a moulding almost indispensable in all combinations of mouldings. It is used to change the flexure of mouldings, and for margins, bands, &c.

ARCHES.

J K N O R S V, Plate XLII, represent the various formation of arches in the different styles of architecture.

W is the imaginary basket represented in accordance with the incident which is said to have given rise to the Corinthian Order.

Y represents a Turkish minaret, and shows the character of the Turkish architecture.

L L L represent three examples of Egyptian columns.

X exhibits a perspective view of a buttress and pinnacle in the Gothic style of building.

P shows an elevation in the Chinese style of architecture.

GLOSSARY OF TECHNICAL TERMS.

Aaron's Rod; an ornamental figure, representing a rod with a serpent twined about it, and called by some, though improperly, *Caduceus* of Mercury.

Abacus; the upper member of the capital of a column, serving as a kind of crown-piece in the Grecian Doric, and a collection of members or mouldings in the Ionic and Corinthian.

Acanthus; a plant, the leaves of which are represented in the capital of the Corinthian Order, &c. *Acanthine* means, ornamented with leaves of the Acanthus.

Accessories; in Architectural composition, those parts or ornaments, either designed or accidental, which are not apparently essential to the use or character of the building.

Acropolis; from the Greek, the highest part of a city; the citadel or fortress.

Alcove; a recess, or part of a chamber, separated by an *estrade*, or partition of columns, and other corresponding ornaments.

Alto-relievo; high relief, that kind or portion of sculpture which projects so much from the surface to which it is attached as to appear nearly isolated. It is therefore used in comparison with Mezzo-relievo, Mean-relief, and in opposition to Basso-relievo or Low-relief.

Amphitheatre; a spacious edifice, of a circular or oval form, in which the combats or shows of antiquity were exhibited.

Ancones; ornaments depending from the corona of Ionic doorways, &c. The *trusses* or *consoles,* or brackets, sometimes employed in the dressings of apertures, as an apparent support to the cornice, upon the flanks of the architrave.

Angels; brackets or carbels, with the figures or heads of angels.

Angle-Bar; the upright bar of a window, constructed on a polygonal plan, standing at the meeting of any two planes of the sides.

Angle-Rafter; in carpentry, otherwise Hip-rafter.

Annulet or *Fillet;* a small, square member in the Doric capital, under the quarter-round. It is also used to imply a narrow, flat moulding, common to the various parts of the column, particularly their bases, capitals, &c.

Antes; a species of pilasters common in the Grecian temples, but differing from pilasters, in general, both in their capitals and situation.

Aerial Perspective; the representation of objects weakened and diminished in proportion to their distance from the eye.

Arcade; an aperture in a wall with an arched head. It also signifies a range of apertures with arched heads. Arcades are frequently constructed as porticoes, instead of colonades, being stronger and less expensive. In the construction, care must be taken that the piers be sufficiently strong to resist the pressure of the arches, particularly those at the extremities; the arcades of the Romans were seen in triumphal arches, in theatres, amphitheatres, and aqueducts, and frequently in temples. They are common in the piazzas and squares of modern cities, and may be employed, with great propriety, in the courts of palaces, &c.

Arch; a part of a building supported at its extremities only, and concave towards earth or horizon: but arches are either circular, elliptical, or *straight;* the last being so termed, but improperly, by workmen. The terms *arch* and *vault* properly differ only in this, that the arch expresses a narrower, and the vault a broader piece of the same kind.

Architectonic; something endowed with the power and skill of building, or calculated to assist the architect.

Architrave; a beam—-that part of an entablature which lies immediately upon the capital or head of the column.

B.

Balcony; (from the French *Balcon,*) an open gallery projecting from the front of a building, and commonly constructed of iron or wood. When a portico or porch is surmounted with a balcony, it is commonly of stone with iron or wood.

Baluster; a small kind of column or pillar, belonging to a *balustrade.*

Balustrade; a range of *balusters* supporting a cornice, and used as a parapet or screen, for concealing a roof or other object.

Bande or *Band;* a narrow, flat surface, having its face in a vertical plane; hence, *Bandelet,* a little band; any flat moulding or fillet.

Base; the lowest part of a figure or body, and finish of rooms, &c.

Bay - Window; a window projecting from the front in two or more planes, and not forming the segment of a circle.

Bearing - Wall or *Partition ;* in a building, a wall resting upon the solid, and supporting some other part, as another wall, &c.

Belfry; the part of a steeple in which the bells are hung.

Belvedere; a turret, look-out, or observatory, commanding a fine prospect, and generally very ornamental.

Bow - Window; a window forming the segment of a circle.

Buffet; an ornamented cupboard or cabinet for plate, glasses, china, &c.

Buttery; a store-room for provisions.

C.

Campana; the body of the Corinthian capital.

Campanæ or *Campanula,* or *Guttæ;* the drops of the Doric architrave.

Campanile; ancient name for a belfry.

Cant-Moulding; a beveled surface, neither perpendicular to the horizon, nor to the vertical surface to which it may be attached.

Cap; in joinery, the uppermost of an assemblage of parts—as the capital of a column, the cornice of a door, &c.

Caryatidæ, or *Caryatides;* so called from the Caryatides, a people of Caria; sashes or glass frames, an order of columns or pilasters under the figure of women dressed in long robes, after the manner of the Carian people, and serving to support an entablature. This order is styled the *Caryatic.*

Case of a Door; the frame in which the door is hung.

Casements; sashes or glass frames opening on hinges, and revolving upon one of the vertical edges.

Castellated; built in imitation of an ancient castle.

Catacomb; a subterranean place for the interment of the dead.

Chancel; the communion place, or that part of a Christian church between the altar and balustrade which encloses it.

Chaplet; a small carved or ornamented fillet.

Colonade; a range of columns, whether attached or insulated, and supporting the entablature.

Comparted; divided into smaller parts, or partitioned into smaller spaces.

Conservatory; a superior kind of greenhouse for valuable plants, &c., arranged in beds of earth with ornamented borders.

Console; a bracket or projecting body, shaped like a curve of contrary flexure, scrolled at the ends, and serving to support a cornice, bust, vase, or other ornament. Consoles are also called, according to their form, *ancones* or *trusses, mutules* and *modillions.*

Contour; A French word for *outline.*

Concentograph; An instrument for radiating lines in linear perspective.

Coping; the stones laid on the top of a wall to strengthen and defend it from injury.

Cornucopia; the horn of plenty; represented in

sculpture under the figure of a large horn, out of which issue fruits, flowers, grain, &c.

Corridor; a long gallery or passage around a building, and leading to the several apartments.

Coupled Columns; those disposed in pairs, so as to form a narrow and wide interval alternately.

Cove; any kind of concave moulding; also, the concavity of a vault. Hence, a coved and flat ceiling of which the section is a part of a circle, springing from the walls, and rising to a flat surface.

Crockets; in the pointed style of architecture, the small ornaments placed equidistantly along the angles of pediments, pinnacles, &c.

Crosetts in Decoration; the trusses or consoles on the flanks of the architrave, under the cornice.

Crown; the uppermost mouldings of a cornice, including the corona, &c. In an arch, its most elevated line or point.

Cupola; a dome, arched roof, or turret.

D.

Demi, or *Semi,* or *Hemi,* signifies one-half. Hence, Semicircle, Hemisphere, &c.

Demi-relievo; in carving or sculpture, denotes that the figure rises one half from the plane. See *Alto-relievo.*

Die of a pedestal; the part comprehended between the base and cornice.

Distemper; in painting, the working up of colors with something besides mere water or oil, as size, or other glutinous or unctious substances.

Ditriglyph; having two triglyphs over an inter-column.

Double-hung sashes; in joinery, those of which the window contains two, and each movable by means of weight and lines.

Dove-tailing; in joinery, a method of fastening one piece of wood to another, by projecting bits cut in the form of dove-tails in one piece, and let into corresponding hollows in another.

Drops; in ornamental architecture, small pendant cylinders, or frustrums of cones attached to a surface vertically, with the upper ends touching a horizontal surface, as in the cornice of the Doric Order.

Drum, or *Vase,* of the Corinthian and Composite capitals; the solid part, to which the ornaments are attached.

Dwarf-Walls; those of less height than the story of a building.

Dye; the plain part of pedestal between the base and cornice.

E.

Eaves; the margin or edge of a roof, overhanging the walls.

Embattled; a building with a parapet having embrasures, and therefore resembling a battery or castle.

Estrade; a French word for a public walk. In a room, a small elevation of the floor, frequently encompassed with a rail or alcove.

F.

Facade; the face or front of a building.

Falling-Moulds; in joinery, the moulds which are to be applied to the vertical sides of the rail-piece, in order to form, the back and under surface of the rail and finish the squaring.

Flyers; steps of which the treads are all parallel.

Fret; a species of ornament commonly composed of straight grooves or channelures at right-angles to each other. The *labyrinth fret* has many turnings or angles, but in all cases the parts are parallel and perpendicular with each other.

Frosted; a species of rustic work representing ice formed by irregular drops of water.

G.

Gable; the triangular part of the wall of a house or building immediately under the roof.

Gothic, more properly, *British* Architecture.

Greek Orders of Architecture; the Doric, Ionic, and Corinthian. See these names respectively.

Groined Ceiling; a cradling constructed of ribs, lathed and plastered.

Grotesque; wildly formed, whimsical; extravagant; of irregular forms and proportions; ludicrous; antic. The term is derived from the figures found in the subterraneous apartments (*grottoes*) in the ancient ruins of Rome, and is hence applied to pieces of sculpture and painting, and to natural scenery; as *grotesque painting; grotesque design.*

H.

Hall; a word commonly denoting a mansion or large public building, as well as the large room at the entrance.

Helix; little scrolls in the Corinthian capital, also called *Urillæ.*

Hem; the projecting and spiral part of the Ionic capital.

Hollow-Wall; a wall built in two thicknesses, leaving a cavity between, which may be either for saving materials, or for preserving a uniform temperature in apartments.

I.

Impost; the footing of an arch, &c.

Inter-column; the open area or space between two columns.

Inter-dentils; the space between two dentils.

Inter-fenestration; the space between windows.

Inter-joist; the space between joists.

Inter-pilaster; the space between pilasters.

Inter-quarter; the space between two quarters.

J.

Jambs; the vertical side of an aperture, as of doors, windows, &c.

Jamb-lining; the lining of a jamb.

Jamp-post; the post fixed on the side of a door, &c., and to which the jamb-lining is attached.

Jamb-stones; in walls, those used in building the sides of an aperture, and of which every alternate stone should have the whole thickness of the wall.

Joggle; the joint of two substances, as of wood, &c., so formed as to prevent their sliding past each other.

K.

Keep; in a castle, the middle or principal tower.

Keyes; in joinery, pieces of wood let transversely into the back of a board, especially when made of several breadths of timber, either by dovetailing or grooving.

L.

Labyrinth; an intricate building, so contrived by its meandering forms as to render it difficult for those who have entered to find the way again. Hence, a *labyrinth-fret,* a fret with many turnings, which was a favorite ornament with the ancients.

Lancet-Arch; the same as *pointed arch.*

Lantern; a turret raised above the roof, with windows round the sides, constructed for lighting an apartment beneath.

Lintels; in carpentry and in masonry, pieces of wood or stone over apertures in a wall.

Lobby; a small hall or waiting room, or the entrance into a principal apartment.

Luthern; a kind of window, over the cornice, in the roof of a building, formed perpendicularly over the naked of the wall, for the purpose of illuminating the upper story. They are denominated according to their forms, as square, semicircular, bull's-eyes, &c.

M.

Mansion; a large dwelling-house or habitation; the chief house of a manor, &c.

Mantels of fire-places; the embellishments of furniture of a fire-place.

Member; any part of an edifice or of a moulding.

Meros; the middle part of a triglyph.

Metope; in the Doric frieze, the square piece or interval between the triglyphs, or between one triglyph and another. The metopes are sometimes left naked, but are more commonly adorned with sculpture. When there is less space than the common metope, which is square, as at the corner of the frieze, it is called a *semi,* or *demi-*metope.

Mezzo-relievo, or *Demi-relievo;* sculpture in half relief.

Minaret; a Turkish steeple with a balcony.

Monotriglyph; having only one triglyph between two adjoining columns; the general practice in the Grecian Doric.

Mosaic, or *Mosaic Work;* an assemblage or combination of small pieces of marble, glass, stones, &c., of various colors and forms, cemented, on a ground so as to imitate paintings. Mosaic work of marble, which is, from its nature, very expensive, may be frequently found in the pavements of temples, palaces, &c.

Museum; originally, a palace at Alexandria, which occupied a considerable part of the city: it was thus named from its being dedicated to the *Muses*, and appropriated to the cultivation of the sciences and of general knowledge.

N.

Naked of a wall or column; the plain surface, in distinction from the ornaments. Thus, the *naked of a wall* is the flat, plain surface that receives the mouldings; and the naked of a column or pilaster is its base surface.

Nave; the body of a church, reaching from the choir or chancel to the principal door.

Neck of a Capital; the space between the channelures and the annulets of the Grecian Doric capital. In the Roman Doric, the space between the astragal and annulet.

Newel; the post at the starting or landing of a stair.

Niche; from an Italian word, signifying a shell; a hollow formed in a wall for receiving a statue, &c. An *Angular Niche* is one formed in the corner of a building; a *Ground Niche*, one having its rise from the ground, without a base or dado.

O.

Obelisk; a quadrangular pyramid, high and slender, raised as a monument of ornament, and commonly charged with inscriptions and ornaments.

Ogee; a moulding of two members, one concave and the other convex. It is otherwise called a *cymatium.*

Oriel Window; a projecting angular window, commonly of a triagonal or pentagonal form, and divided by mullions and transoms into different bays and compartments.

Orthography; an elevation, showing all the parts of a building in true proportion.

Out of Winding; perfectly smooth or even, or forming a true plane.

P.

Palace; a name generally given to the dwellings of kings, princes, bishops, &c.

Palisade; pales or stakes set for an enclosure.

Pantheon; a temple of a circular form, originally Pagan.

Parapet; a dwarf-wall, generally raised to prevent accidents.

Pedestal; a square body of stone or other material, raised to sustain a column, statue, &c. It is, therefore, the base, or lowest part of an order of columns. A *Square Pedestal* is that of which the height and width are equal; a *Double Pedestal*, that which supports two columns, and is, therefore, greater in width than height; a *Continued Pedestal* is that which supports a row of columns without any break.

Pediment; an ornament, properly of a low triangular figure, crowning the front of a building, and serving, often, also, as a decoration over doors, windows, and niches. Though the original, and natural form of the pediment be triangular it is sometimes formed as the segment of a circle, and sometimes broke, to let in busts or figures. The pediment consists of its *tympanum* and *cornice.* The tympanum is the panel which may be either plane or ornamented. The cornice crowns this tympanum.

Persians; statues of men, serving instead of columns to support entablatures. They differ from the *Caryatides*, inasmuch as the latter represent women only.

Piazza; a portico or covered walk supported by arches.

Pier; a square pillar, without any regular base or capital.

Pilasters; a pilaster, in Roman architecture, has the same proportion in diameter and mouldings as the column. The Grecian pilaster is generally called *Ante*, and differs in diameter, base, and capital. A *Demi-pilaster* is one that supports an arch.

Pillar; a column of an irregular make — not formed according to rules, but of arbitrary proportions; free or isolated in every part, and always deviating from the measures of regular columns. This is the distinction of the *pillar* from the *column.* A square pillar is commonly called a *pier.* A butting pillar is called a butment or body of masonry, erected to prop, or to sustain, the thrust of a vault, arch, &c.

Pinnacle; the top of the roof of a building, terminating in a point.

Plinth; the square piece under the mouldings in the bases of columns. The *plinth* terminates the column with its base at the bottom, as the *abacus* does with its capital at the top: but the abacus in the Tuscan Order being plain, square, and massy, has been called the plinth of that capital. The plinth of a statue, &c., is a base serving to support it and its pedestal.

Pointed-Arch; an arch so pointed at the top as to resemble the point of a lance.

Pointed Architecture; that style vulgarly called *Gothic,* but more properly *English.*

Porch; the kind of vestibule at the entrance of temples, halls, churches, &c.

Portail; the face of a church, on the side in which the great door is formed; also the gate of a palace, castle, &c.

Portal; a little gate when there are two of a different size; also, a kind of arch of joiner's work before a door.

Portico; a covered walk, porch, or piazza, supported by columns.

Profile; the figure or draught of a building, &c.; also, the general contour or outline.

Projecture; the out-jetting, or prominence, which the mouldings and other ornaments have beyond the naked of the walls, &c.

Pyramid; a solid, massive structure, which, from a square, triangular, or other base, rises, diminishing to a vertex or point.

Q.

Quadrangle; a figure having four sides and four angles: a square is, therefore, a regular quadrangle, and a trapezium an irregular one.

Quirk; a recess member in mouldings.

R.

Raking Moulding; a moulding whose arrises are inclined to the horizon in any given angle.

Rotondo or *Rotunda;* a common name for any circular building.

Rubble-Wall; a wall built of unhewn stone, whether with or without mortar.

Rustic-building; one constructed in the simplest manner, and apparently more agreeably to the face of nature than the rules of art. Rustic work and rustic quoins are commonly used in the basement part of a building.

S.

Saloon; a spacious, lofty, and elegant hall or apartment, vaulted at the top, and generally having two ranges of windows; a state-room common in the palaces of Italy.

Sarcophagus; a tomb of stone, in general, highly decorated, and used by the ancients to contain the dead bodies of distinguished personages.

Sesspool, or *Cesspool;* a deep hole or well under the mouth of a drain, for the reception of sediment, &c., by which the drain might be choked.

Sewer; a common drain or conduit for conveying foul water, &c.

Shaft of a column; the part between the base and capital.

Sham-door; in joinery, a panel of framework that appears like a door, but does not open.

Soffita, or *Soffit;* any timber ceiling, formed of cross beams of flying cornices, the square compartments or panels of which are enriched with sculpture or painting. *Soffit* also means the underside of an architrave, and that of the corona or drip, &c., also, the horizontal undersides of the heads of apertures, as of doors and windows.

Span of an Arch; the extremities of the inner or outer sides, as the case may be.

Sphinx; a favorite ornament in Egyptian Architecture, representing the monster, half woman and half beast, said to have been born of Typhon and Echidna.

Square in geometry, but, among workmen, it commonly means that one side or surface is perpendicular to another. In joinery, the work is said to be framed square, when the framing has all the angles of its stiles, rails, and mountings square, without mouldings.

Square of building, is one hundred superficial feet, measured on the surface of the ground.

String-board; in stairing, a board placed next to the well-hole, and terminating the ends of the steps.

Stalactends; ornaments of cylindrical or conical form, depending from the soffit of the cornice in Cottage Architecture.

Surbaces; a horizontal finish around rooms immediately under the windows.

T.

Telamones; a Roman term for the figures of men supporting a cornice.

Terrace; an elevated area for walking upon, and sometimes meaning a balcony.

Terrace-roof; roof flat on the top

Torus; a semi-bead.

Transom; a cross-beam; the horizontal piece framed across a double-lighted window.

Transom-windows; a window or light over a door, &c. Improperly called fan-lights.

Trellis-work; reticulated or net-like framing, made of thin bars of wood.

Triglyph, or *Trigliph;* an ornament in the frieze of a Doric entablature.

Tuscan Order; an order in architecture invented in Tuscany.

Tympanum, or *Tympan;* see *Pediment.* Tympan also signifies the panel of a door and the die of a pedestal.

V.

Valley; the internal angle of two inclined sides of a roof.

Valley-rafter; a rafter at the internal angle of a roof. The valley-board is the board fixed upon this rafter for the leaden gutter to lie upon.

Vault; an interior concavity extending over two parallel opposite walls. The axis of a vault is the same as the axis of a geometrical solid. The *Reins* of a vault are the sides or walls which sustain the arch.

Venetian Door; a door lighted on each side.

Venetian Window; a window having three separate apertures.

Ventiduct; a passage or place for wind or fresh air.

Volute; the scroll or principal ornament of the Ionic capital.

W.

Well-hole of Stairs; the entire space occupied by a stair, as also the opening between front strings, either straight or circular.

Water-table; the uppermost stone and shield to a wall.

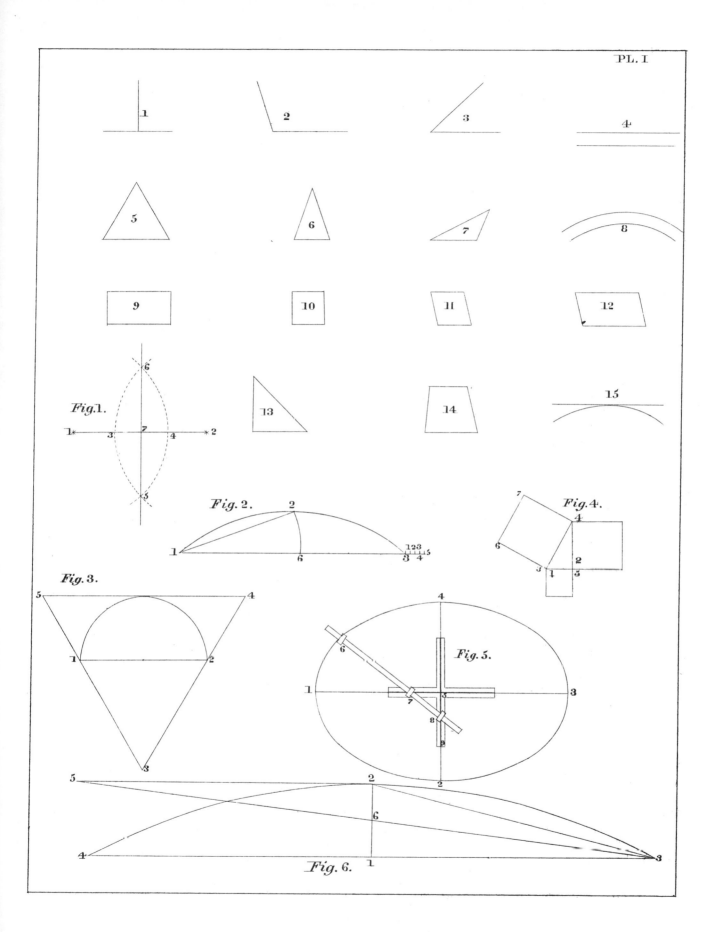

Fig.1.

Fig.2.

Fig.3.

Fig.4.

Fig.5.

Fig.6.

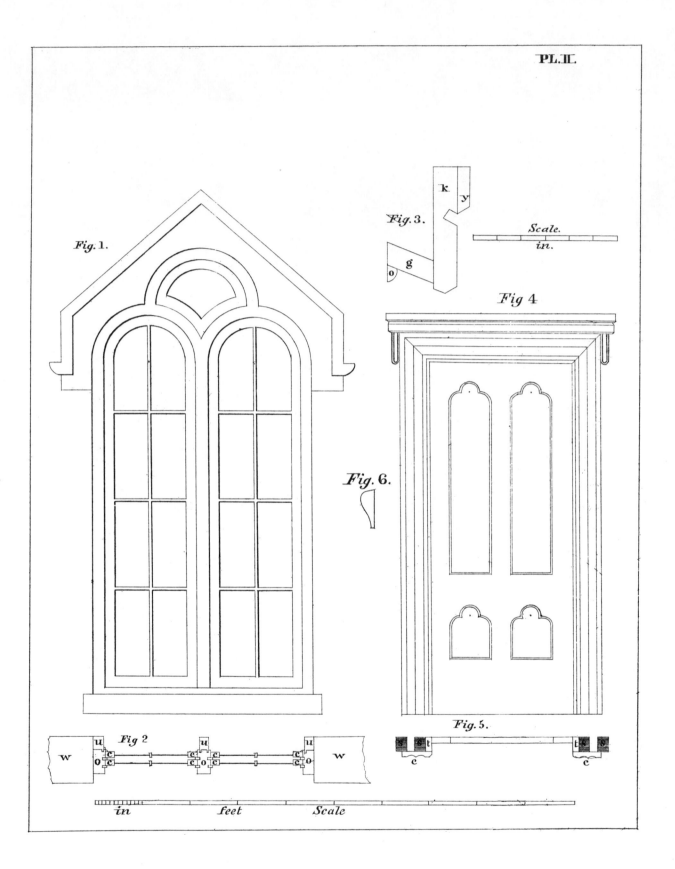

Fig. 1.

Fig. 3.

k
y
o g

Scale.
in.

Fig 4

Fig. 6.

Fig 2

u
w
c
o c

u
c c
o c
c c

u
c
o c
w

Fig. 5.

s s t
c

t s s
c

in   feet   Scale

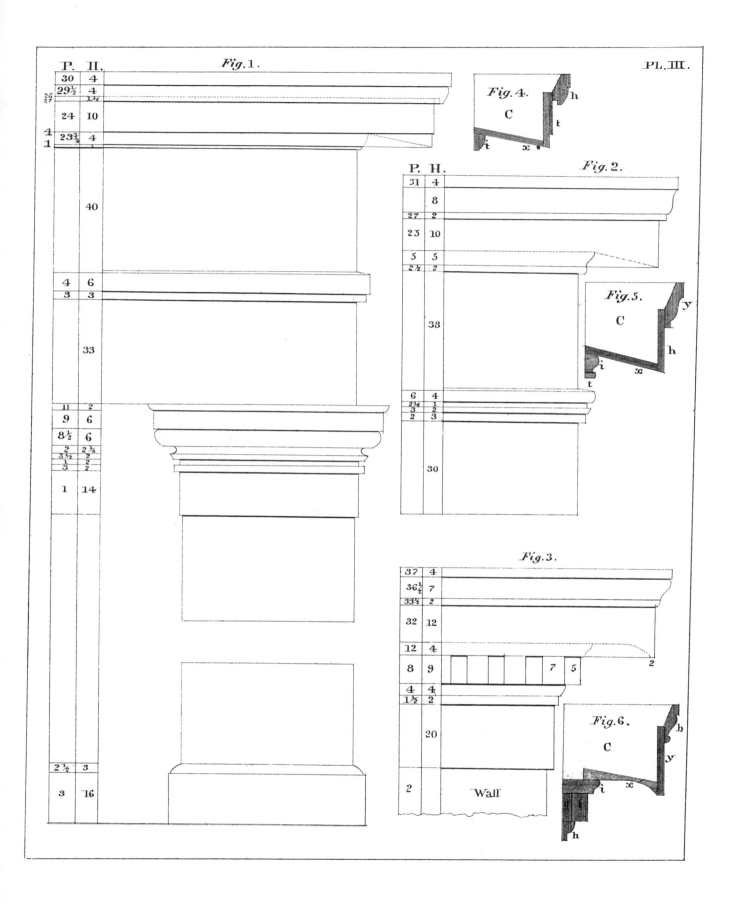

PL.III.

Fig.1.

Fig.2.

Fig.3.

Fig.4.

Fig.5.

Fig.6.

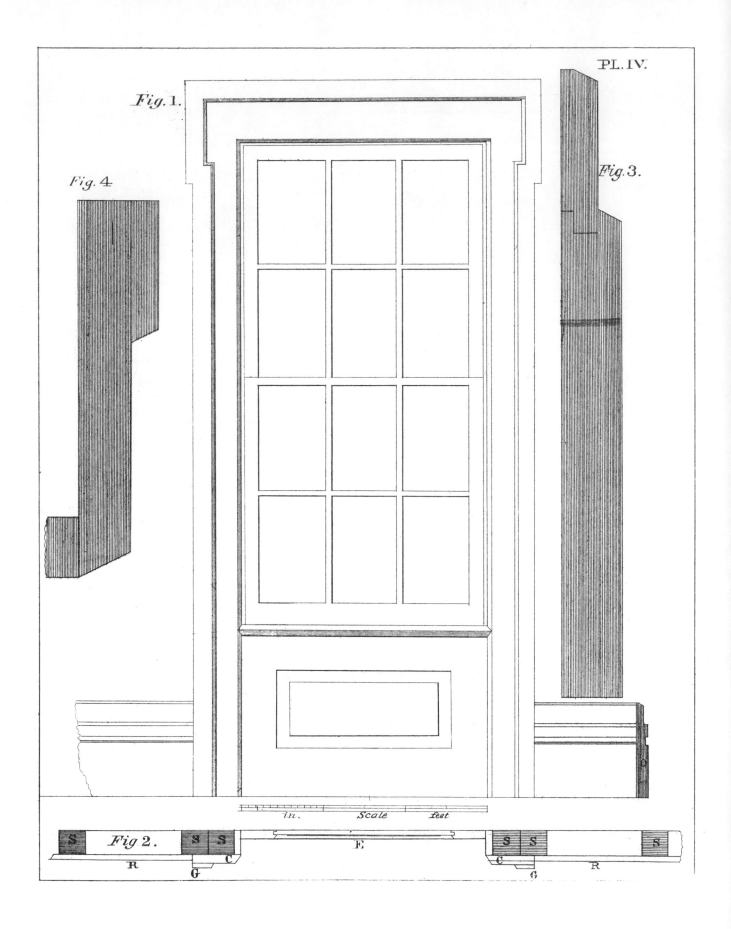

PL. IV.

Fig. 1.

Fig. 4

Fig. 3

Fig 2.

S   S S   E   S S   S

R   C G   C G   R

in.   Scale   feet

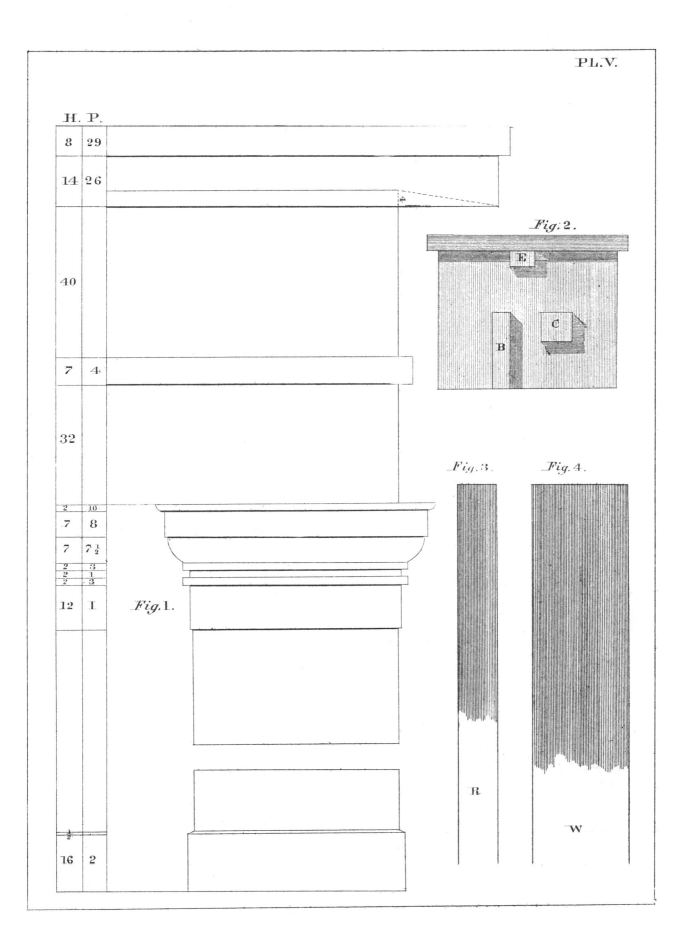

Fig: 2.

Fig. 3.

Fig. 4.

Fig. 1.

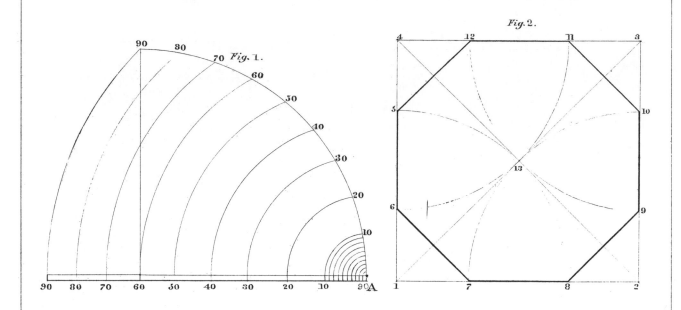

Fig. 1.

Fig. 2.

Fig. 3.

Fig. 4.

F.R. SMITH DEL.

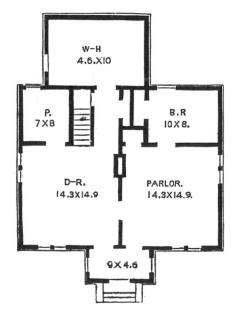

W-H
4.6.X10

P.
7X8

B.R
10X8.

D-R.
14.3X14.9

PARLOR.
14.3X14.9.

9X4.6

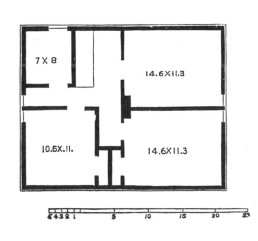

7X8

14.6X11.3

10.6X.11.

14.6X11.3

PL. VIII.

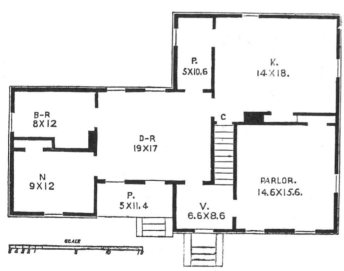

P.
5X10.6

K.
14 X 18.

B-R
8X12

D-R
19X17

C

N
9X12

P.
5 XII. 4

V.
6.6X8.6

PARLOR.
14.6X15.6.

SCALE

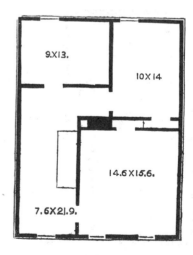

9. X13.

10X 14

14.6 X15.6.

7.6X21.9.

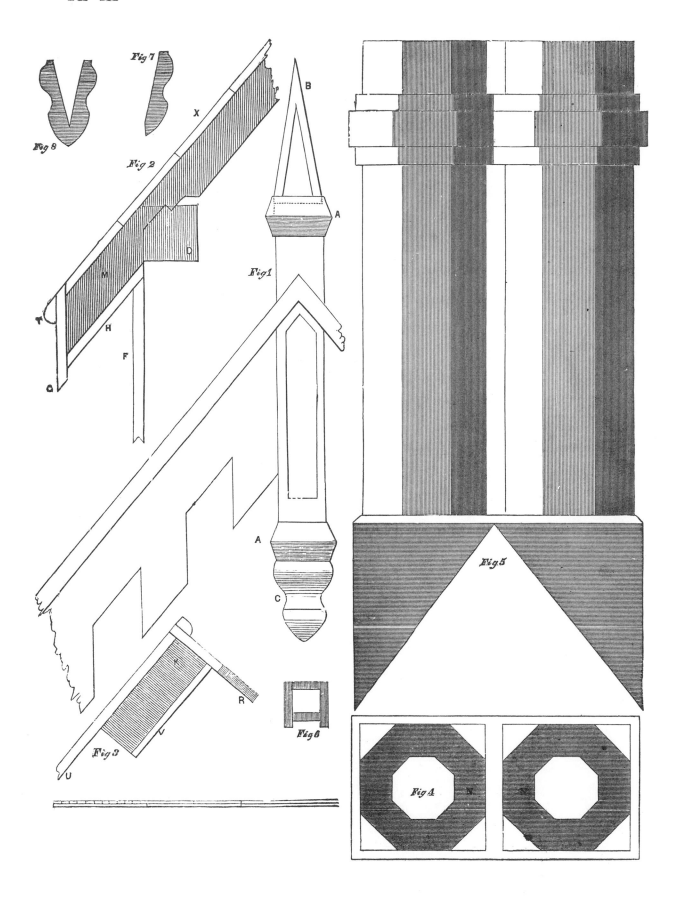

PL IX

Fig 7

Fig 8

Fig 2

Fig 1

Fig 3

Fig 6

Fig 5

Fig 4

Pl. X

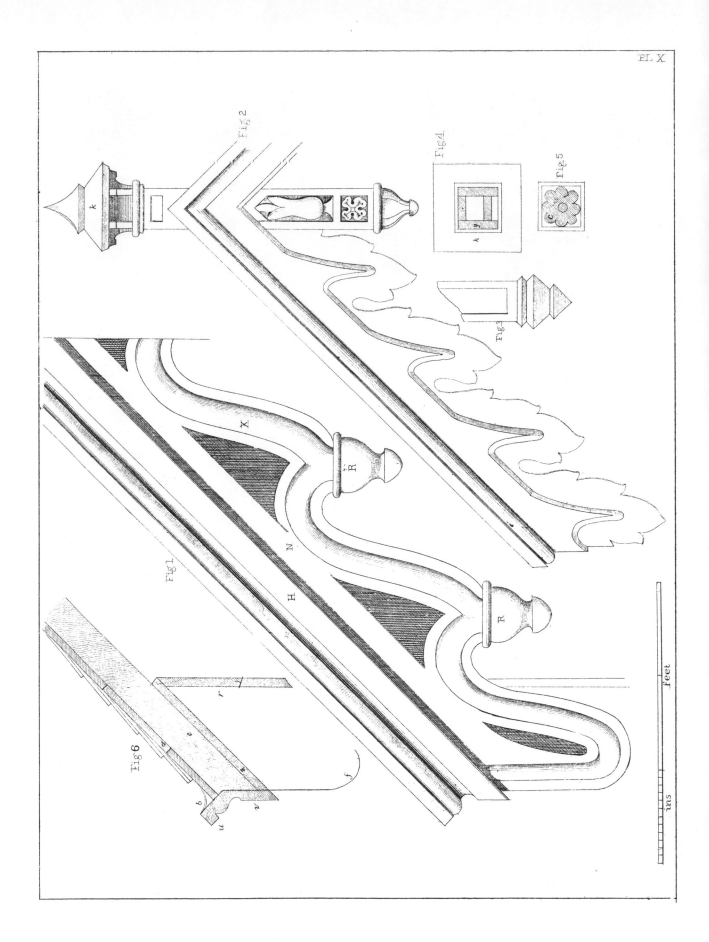

Fig 2

Fig 4

Fig 5

Fig 3

Fig 1

Fig 6

Feet

ins

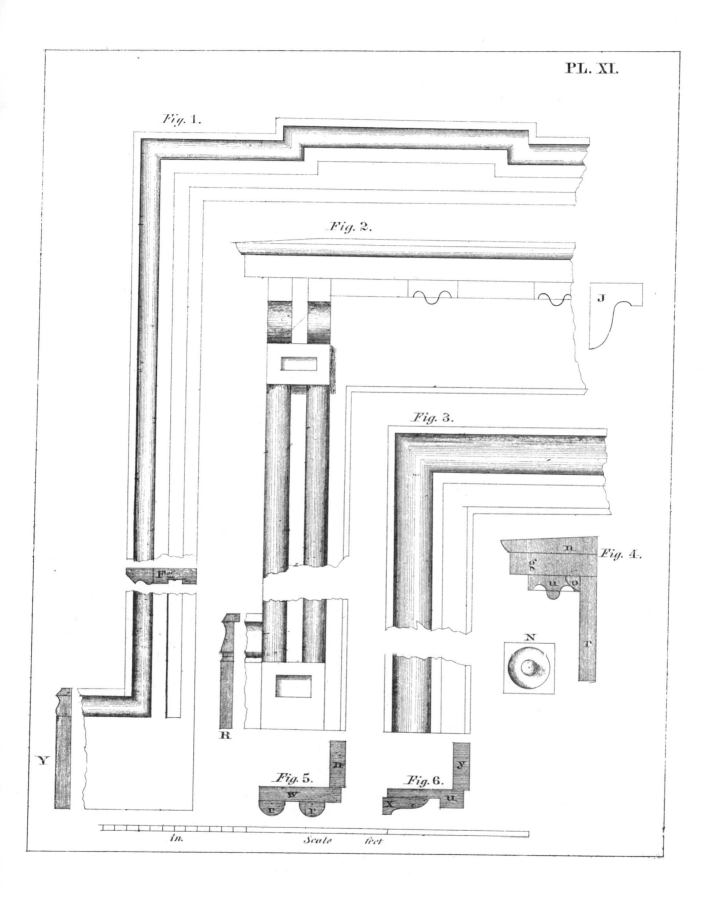

PL. XI.

Fig. 1.

Fig. 2.

Fig. 3.

Fig. 4.

Fig. 5.

Fig. 6.

in.   Scale   feet

BALUSTRADES

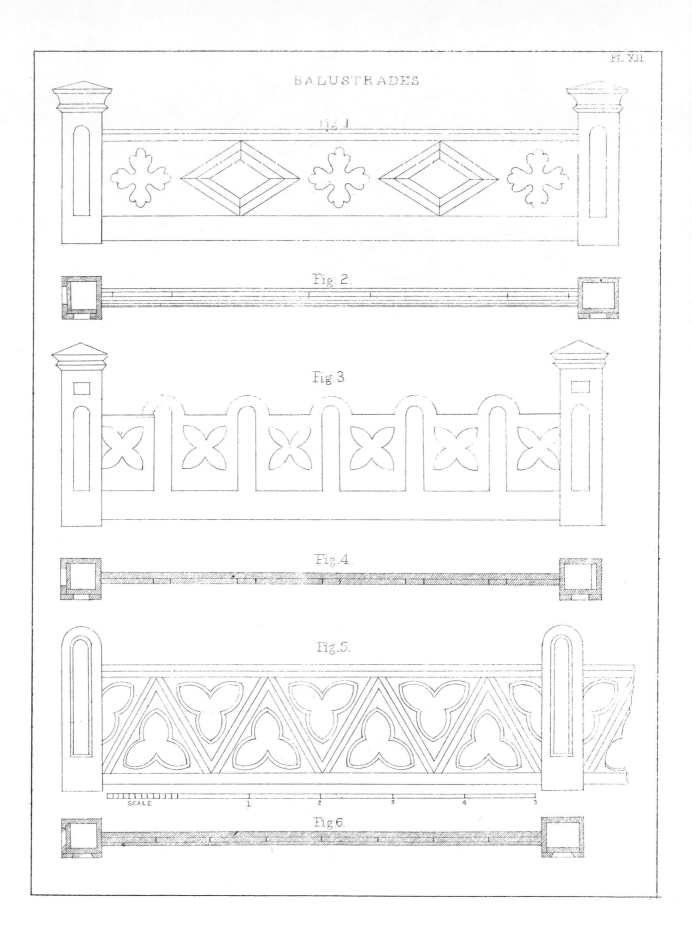

Fig. 1.

Fig. 2.

Fig. 3.

Fig. 4.

Fig. 5.

SCALE   1   2   3   4   5

Fig. 6.

VERANDA COLUMNS

Fig. 1.   Fig. 2   Fig. 3.   Fig. 4   Fig. 5

SCALE   1   2   3   4

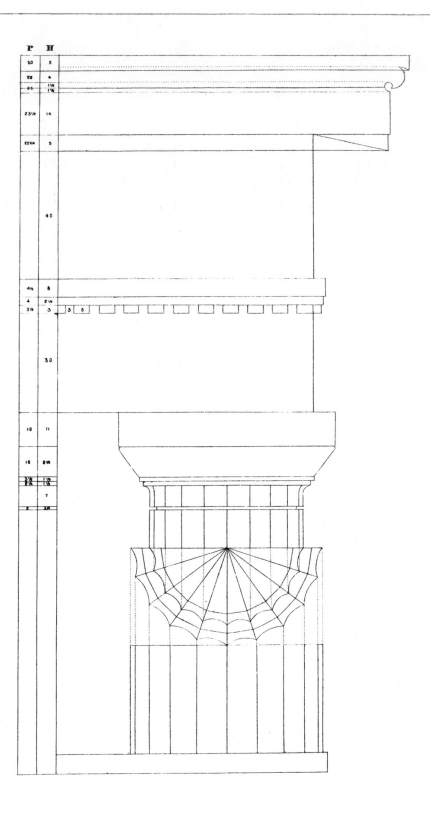

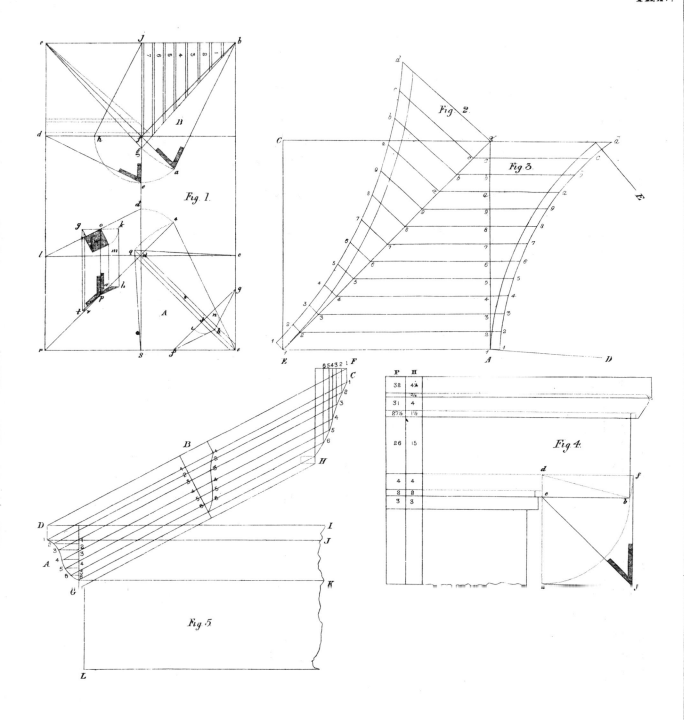

Fig. 1.

Fig. 2.

Fig. 3.

Fig. 4.

Fig. 5.

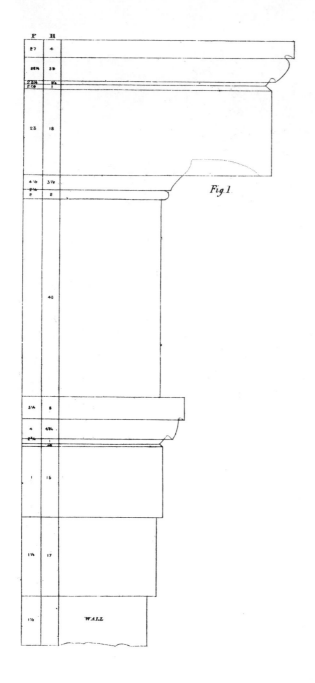

Fig.1

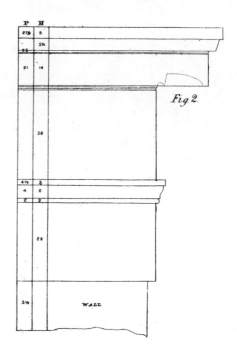

Fig.2

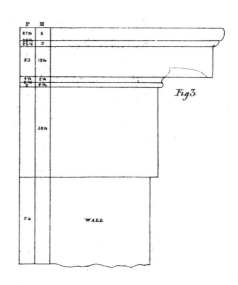

Fig3

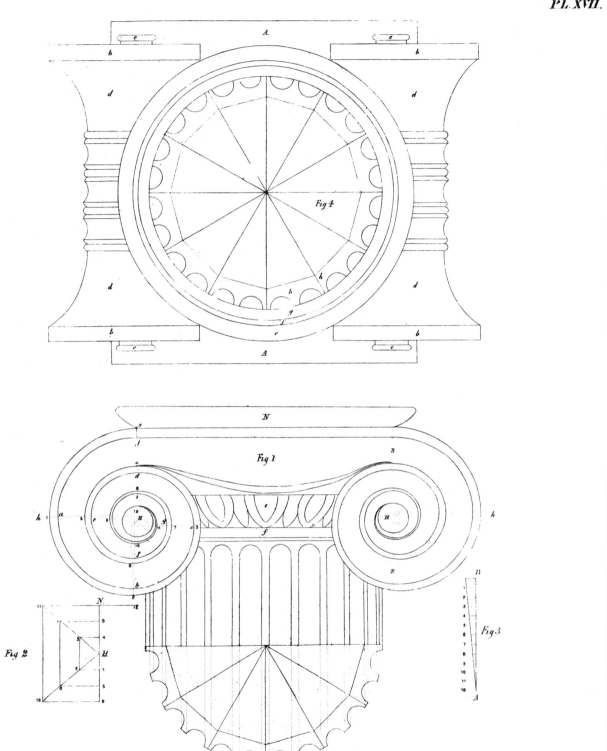

Fig 4

Fig 1

Fig 2

Fig 3

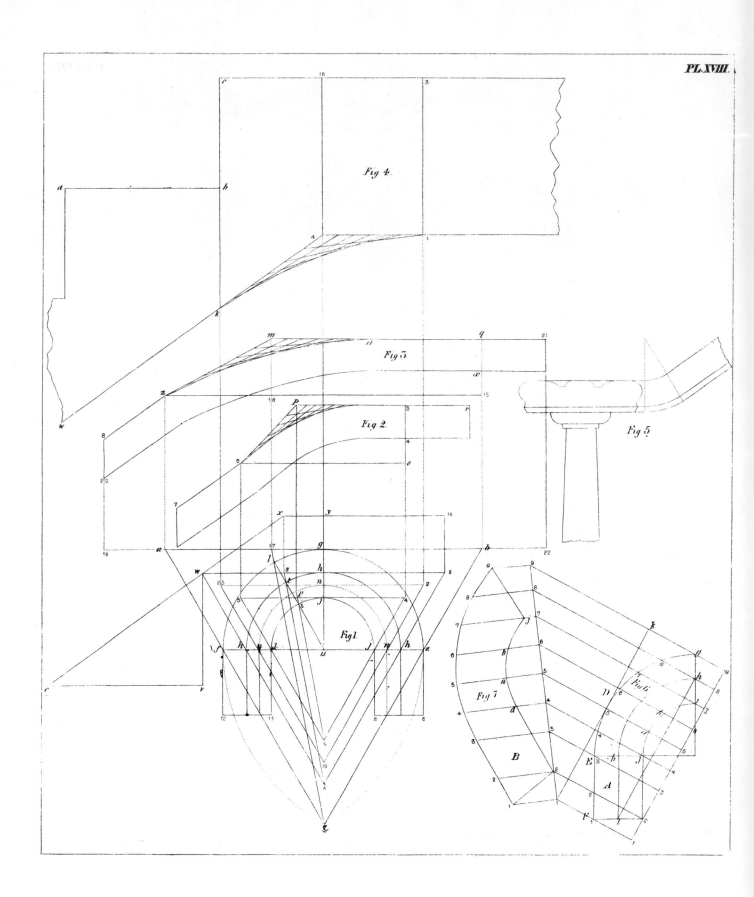

Fig 4.

Fig 3.

Fig 2.

Fig 5.

Fig 1.

Fig 7

Fig 6

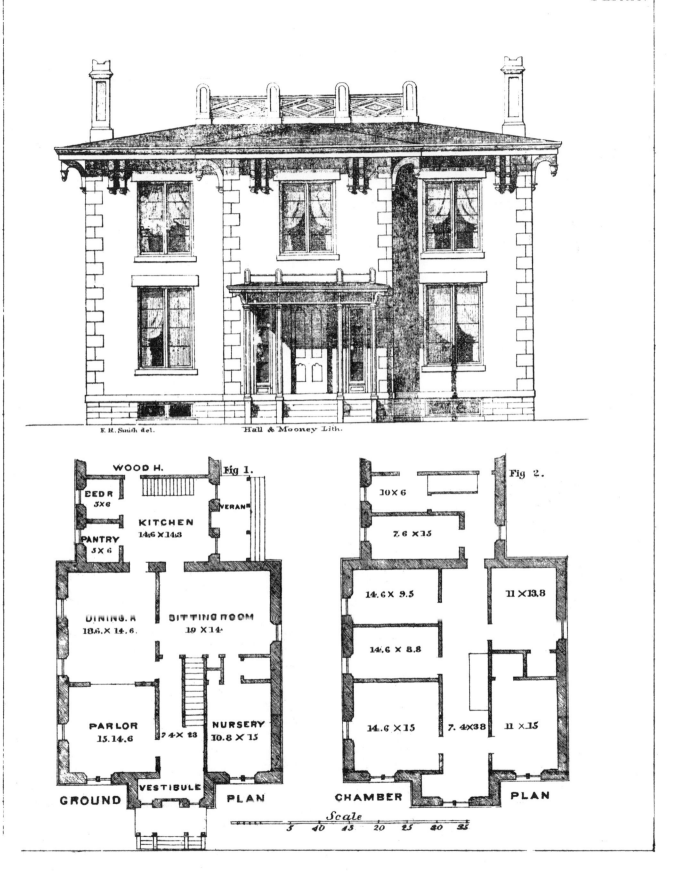

F.R.Smith del.   Hall & Mooney Lith.

Fig 1.

WOOD H.

BED R
5×8

PANTRY
5×6

KITCHEN
14.6 × 14.3

VERAND

DINING. R
18.6.× 14.6.

SITTING ROOM
19 ×14

PARLOR
15. 14.6

7.4× 13

NURSERY
10.8 × 15

VESTIBULE

GROUND   PLAN

Fig 2.

10× 6

7. 6 ×15

14.6 × 9.5

11 ×13.8

14.6 × 8.8

14.6 ×15   7. 4×38   11 ×15

CHAMBER   PLAN

Scale
5   10   15   20   25   30   35

BRACKETS AND CONSOLES.

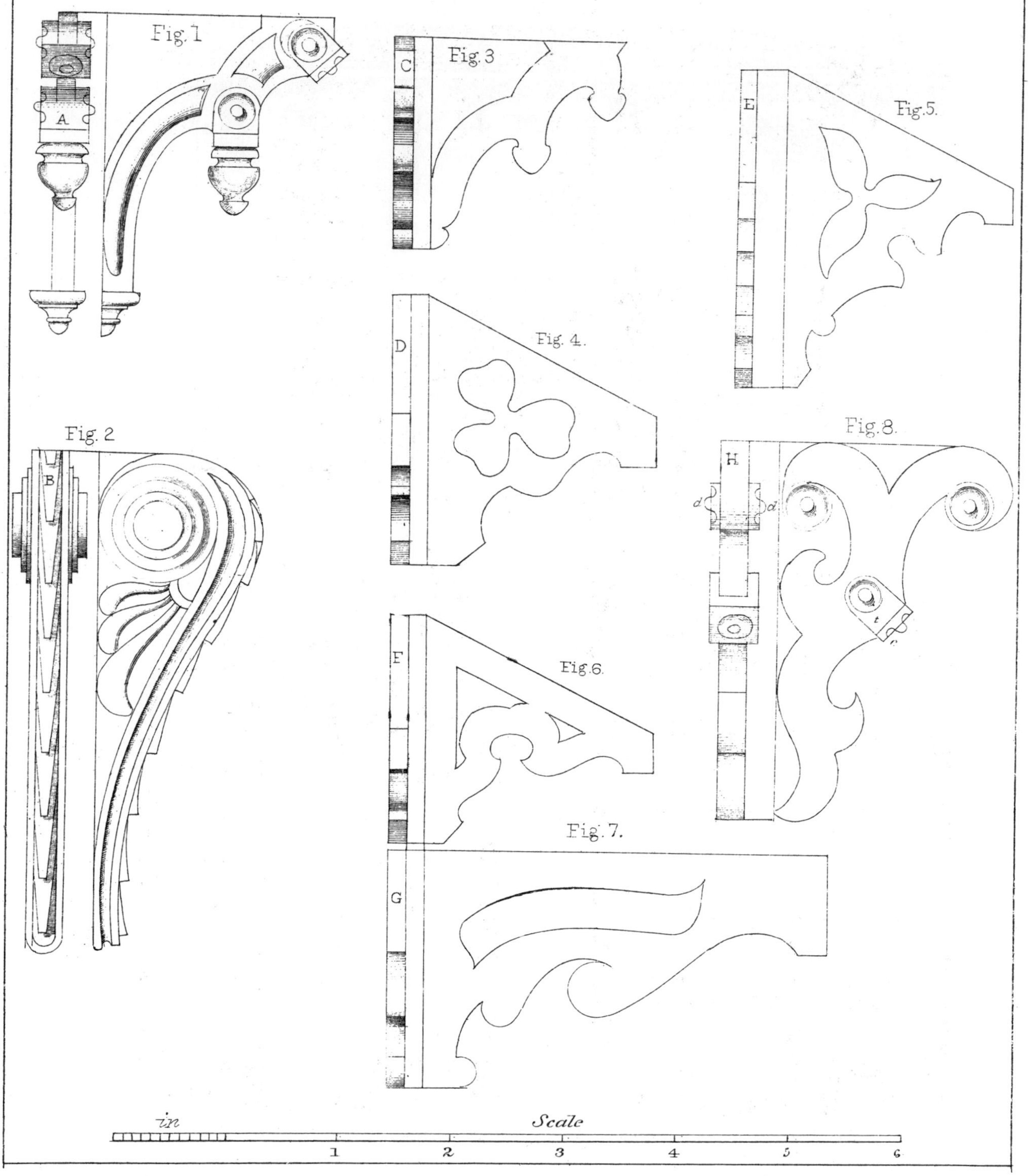

Fig. 1
A
Fig. 2
B
Fig. 3
C
Fig. 4.
D
Fig. 5.
E
Fig. 6.
F
Fig. 7.
G
Fig. 8.
H
d
d
t
c
in
Scale
1
2
3
4
5
6

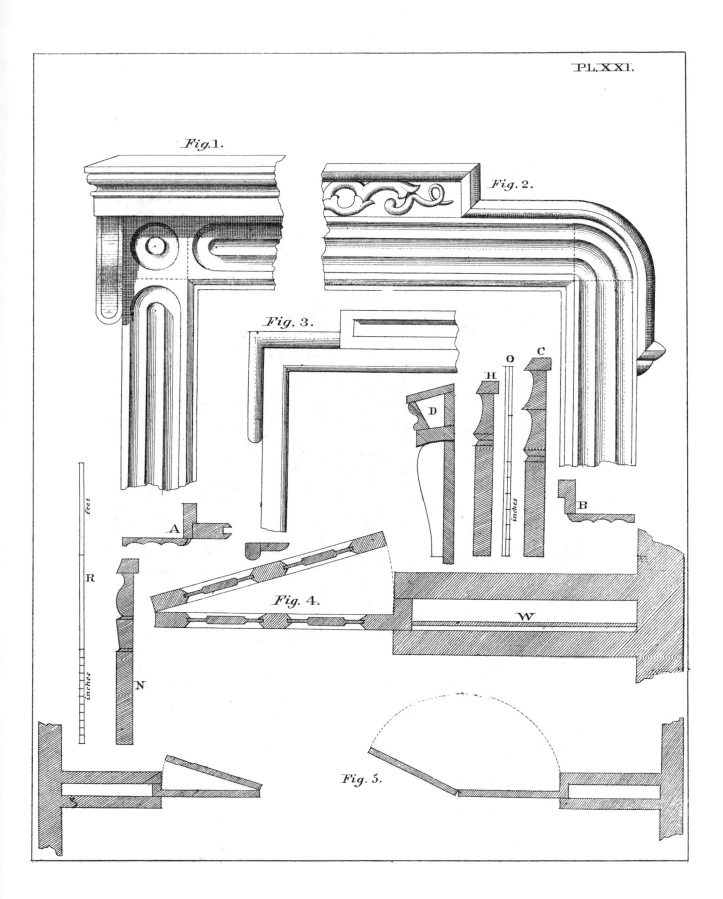

Fig. 1.

Fig. 2.

Fig. 3.

Fig. 4.

Fig. 5.

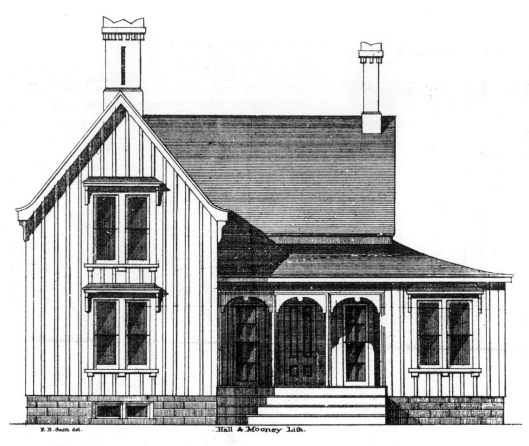

F. R. Smith del.   Hall & Mooney lith.

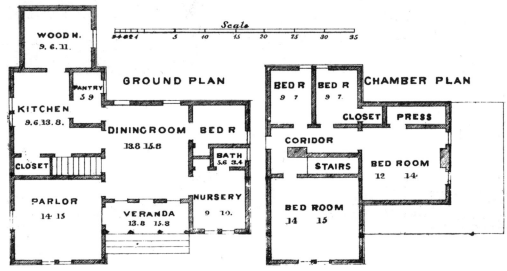

GROUND PLAN

CHAMBER PLAN

WOOD H.
9. 6. 11.

Scale

PANTRY
5 9

KITCHEN
9. 6. 13. 8.

DININGROOM
13.8 15.8

BED R

CLOSET

BATH
5.6 3.4

PARLOR
14 15

VERANDA
13.8 15.8

NURSERY
9 10.

BED R
9 7

BED R
9 7

CLOSET

PRESS

CORIDOR

STAIRS

BED ROOM
12 14

BED ROOM
14 15

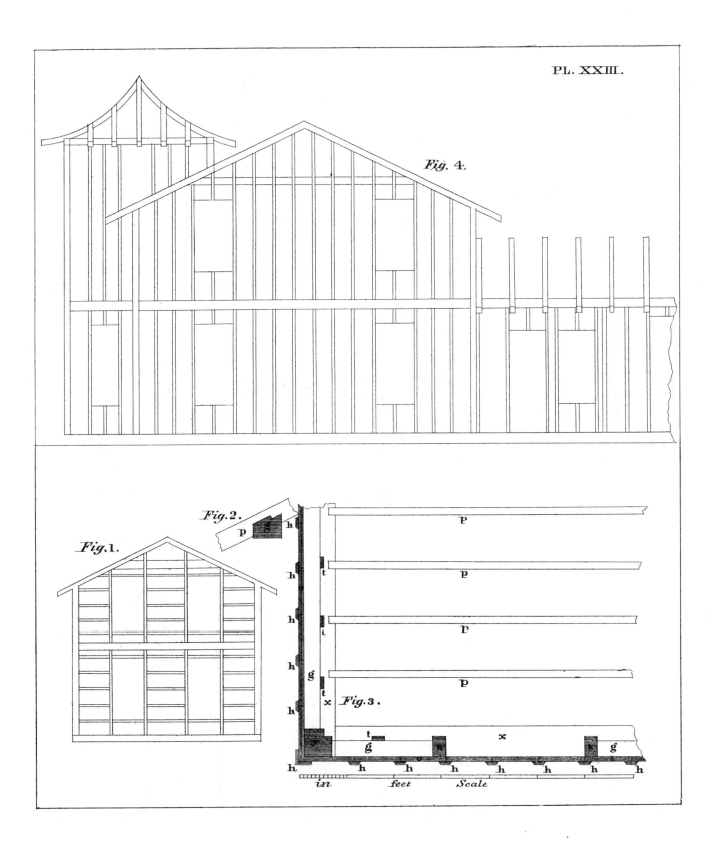

PL. XXIII.

Fig. 4.

Fig. 2.

Fig. 1.

Fig. 3.

in   feet   Scale

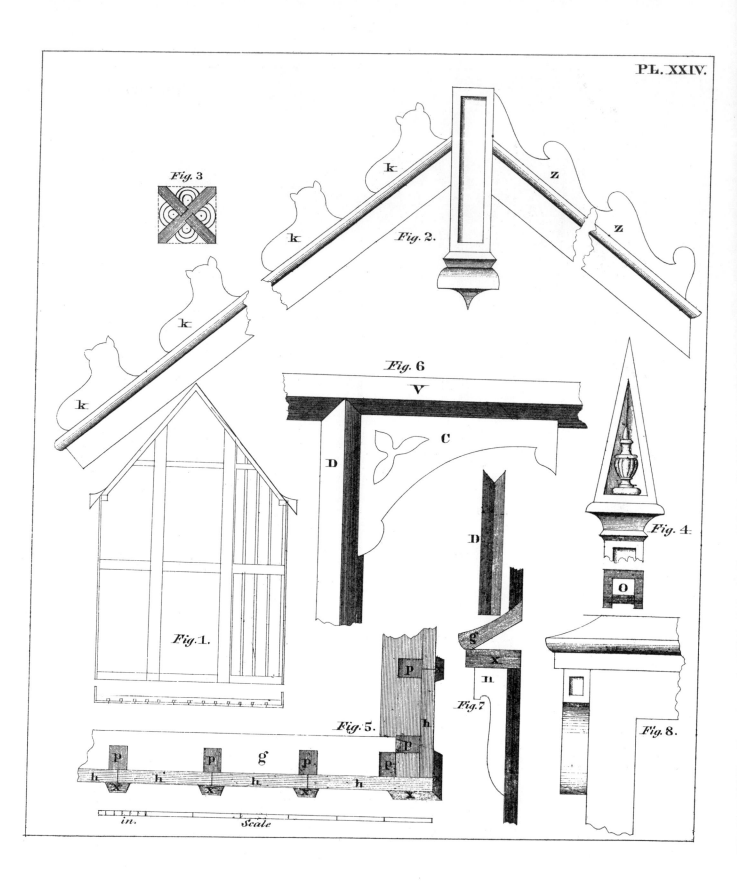

PL. XXIV.

Fig. 3

Fig. 2.

k k k k

z z

Fig. 6

V

C

D D

Fig. 4

O

Fig. 1.

g

x

n

Fig. 7.

Fig. 8.

P

P

h

P

p

h h h h

p p p

g

x x x x

in. Scale

F. R. Smith del.   Hall & Mooney Lith.

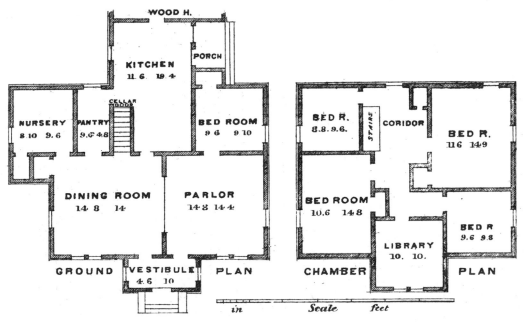

WOOD H.

KITCHEN
11. 6. 19. 4.

PORCH

CELLAR DOOR

NURSERY
8. 10 9. 6

PANTRY
9. 6 4. 8

BED ROOM
9. 6 9. 10

DINING ROOM
14. 8 14

PARLOR
14. 8 14. 4

GROUND   VESTIBULE   PLAN
                4. 6 10

BED R.
8. 8. 9. 6.

STAIRS

CORIDOR

BED R.
11. 6 14. 9

BED ROOM
10. 6 14. 8

LIBRARY
10. 10.

BED R.
9. 6 9. 8

CHAMBER   PLAN

in   Scale   feet

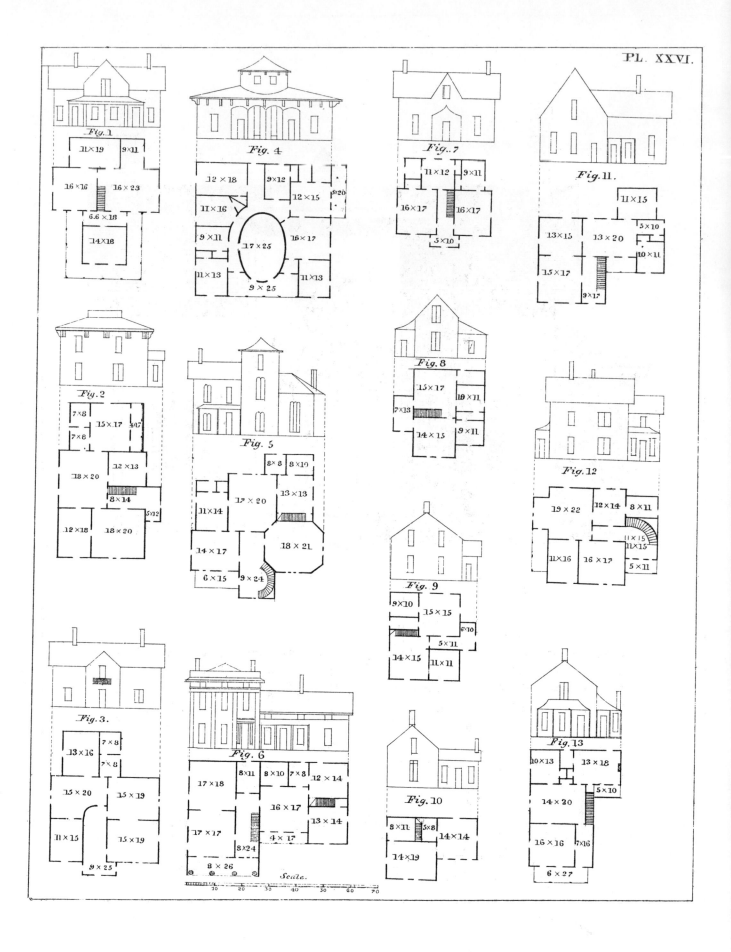

PL. XXVI.

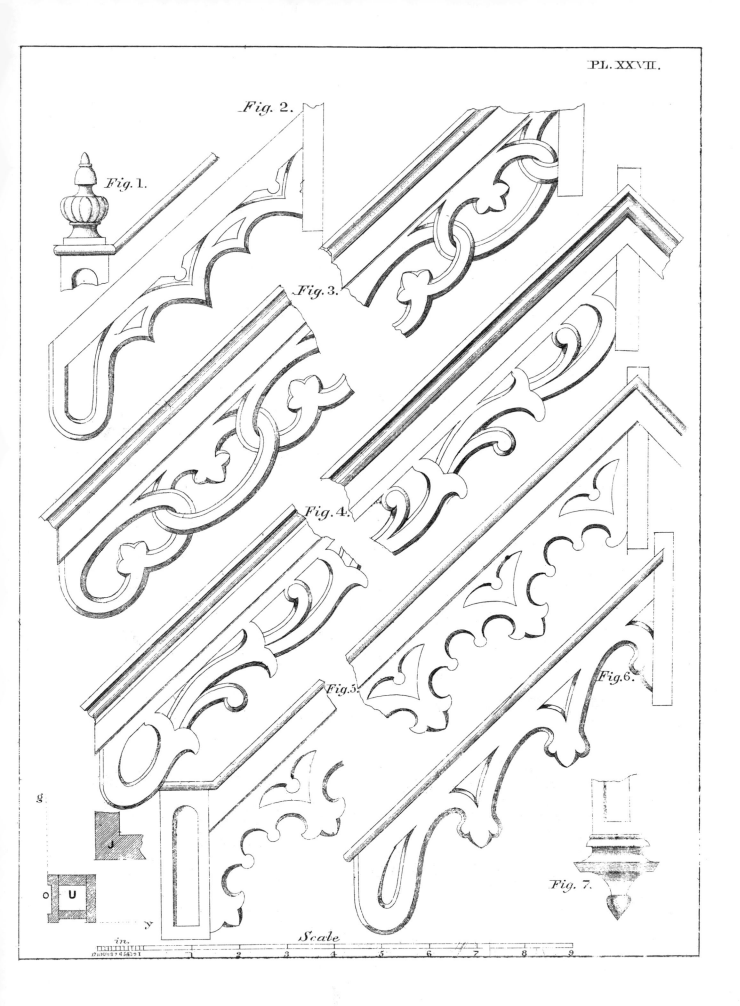

PL. XXVII.

Fig. 2.

Fig. 1.

Fig. 3.

Fig. 4.

Fig. 5.

Fig. 6.

Fig. 7.

g

J

o   U

y

in.

Scale

1   2   3   4   5   6   7   8   9

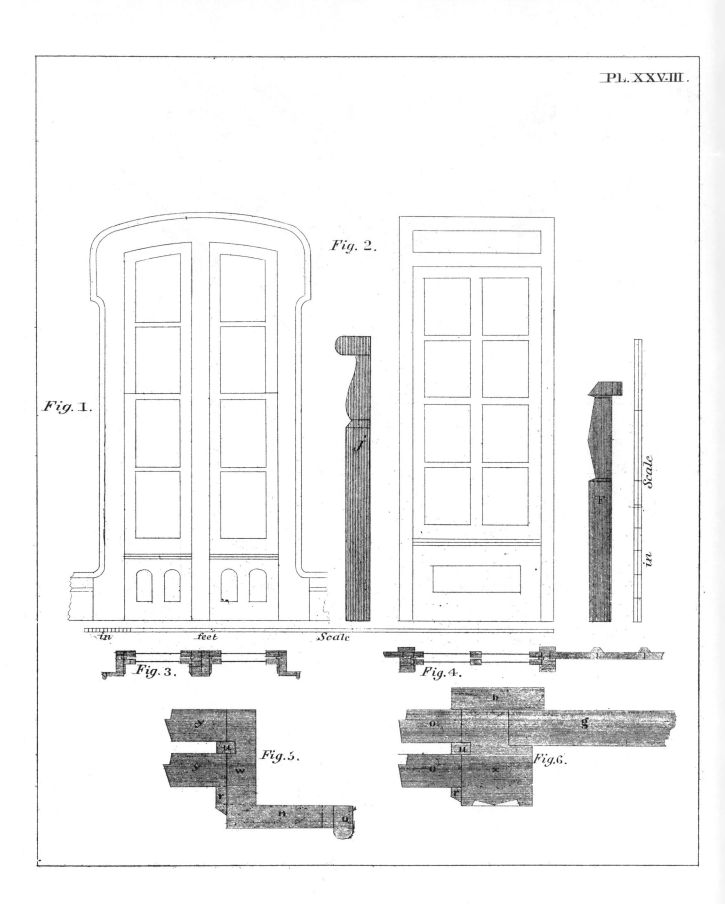

Fig. 2.

Fig. 1.

Scale

in   feet   Scale

Fig. 3.

Fig. 4.

Fig. 5.

Fig. 6.

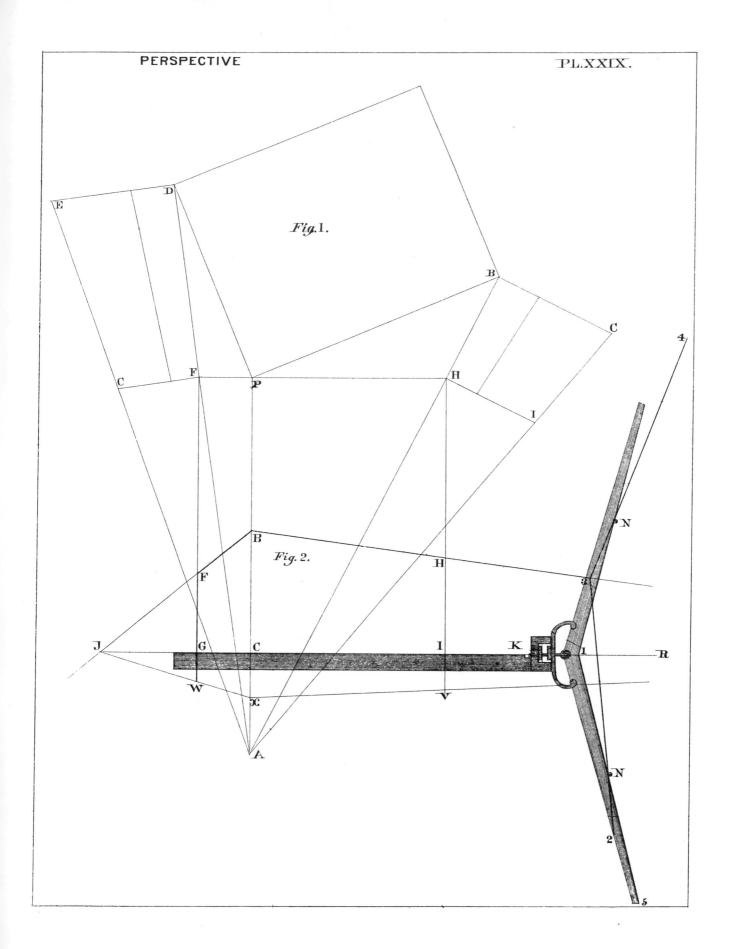

*Fig.*1.

Fig. 2.

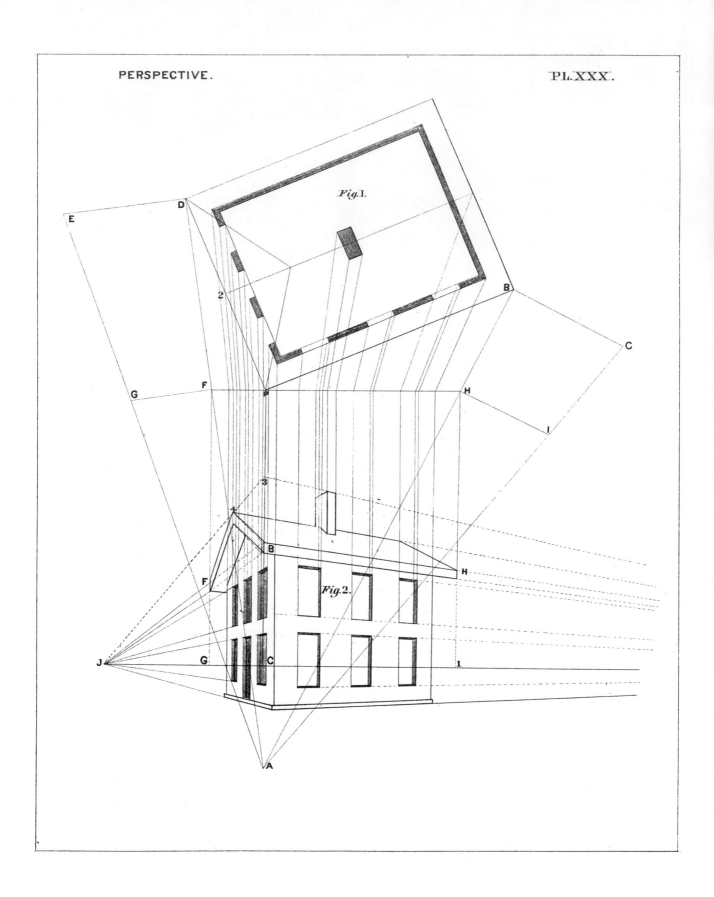

Fig.1.

Fig.2.

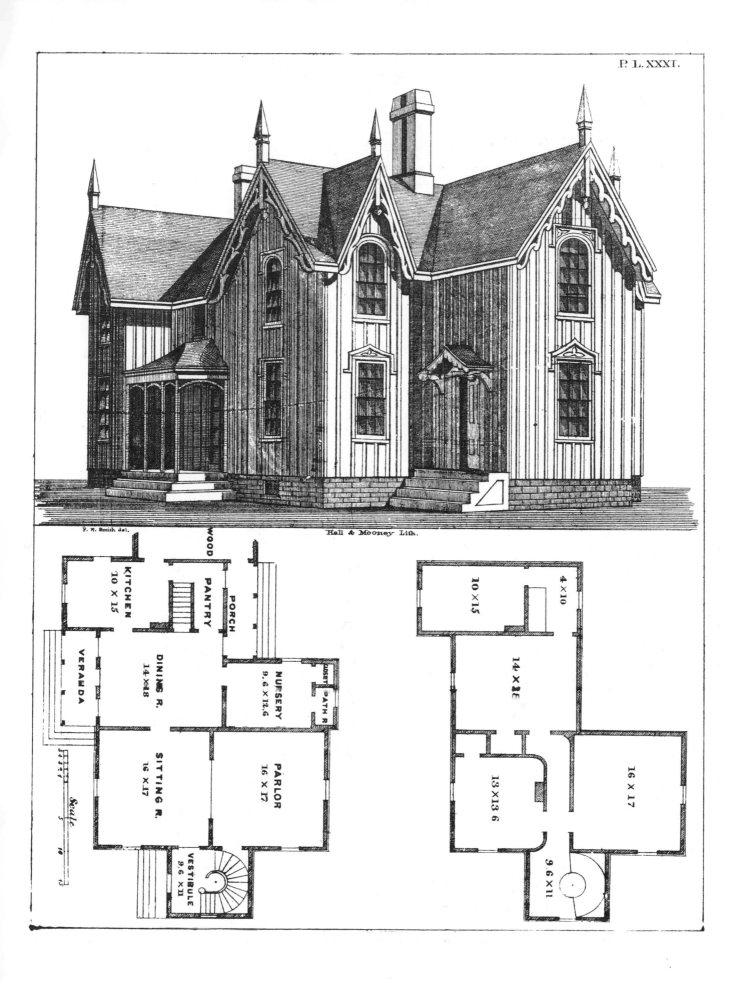

F. R. Smith del.

Hall & Mooney Lith.

KITCHEN
10 × 15

WOOD

PANTRY

PORCH

NURSERY
9. 6 × 12. 6

CLOSET

BATH R

VERANDA

DINING R.
14 ×18

SITTING R.
16 × 17

PARLOR
16 × 17

VESTIBULE
9. 6 × 11

Scale

4 ×10

10 ×15

14 × 16

13 ×13. 6

16 × 17

9. 6 × 11

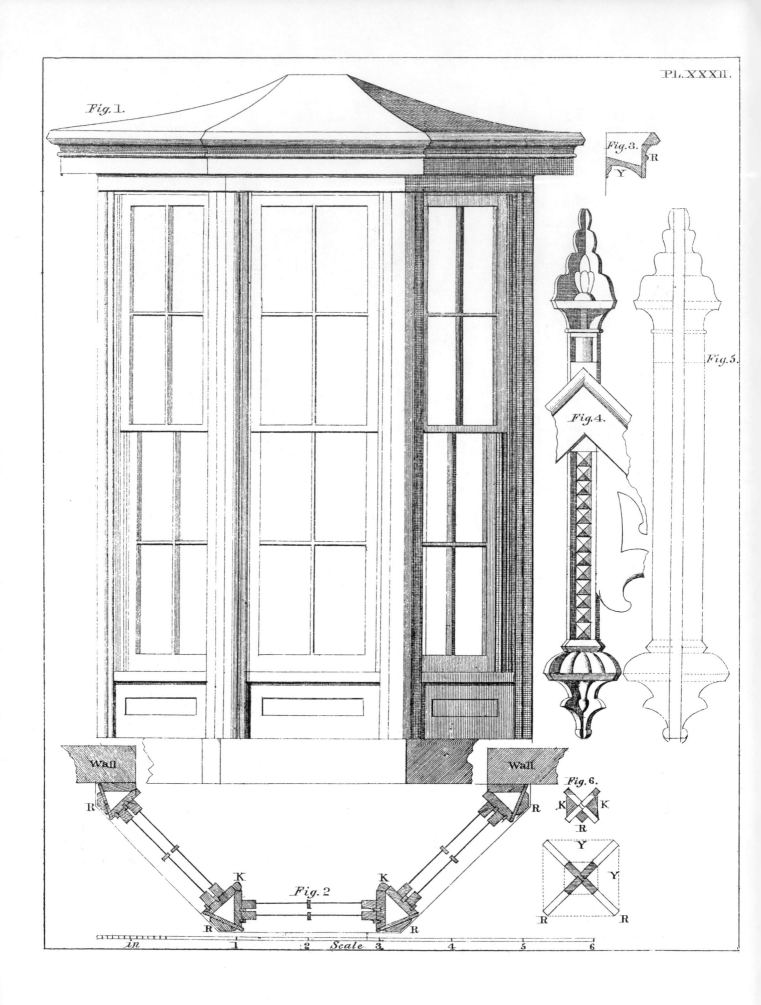

Fig. 1.

Fig. 3.

R

Y

Fig. 4.

Fig. 5.

Wall

Wall

Fig. 6.

R

R

K

K

K

K

R

Y

Y

R

R

K

Fig. 2

R

in   1   2   Scale 3   4   5   6

LP. XXXIII.

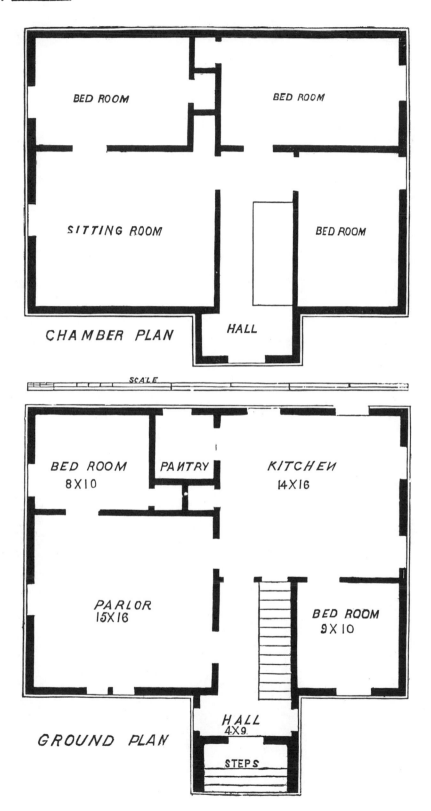

BED ROOM

BED ROOM

SITTING ROOM

BED ROOM

HALL

CHAMBER PLAN

SCALE

BED ROOM
8X10

PANTRY

KITCHEN
14X16

PARLOR
15X16

BED ROOM
9X10

HALL
4X9.

GROUND PLAN

STEPS

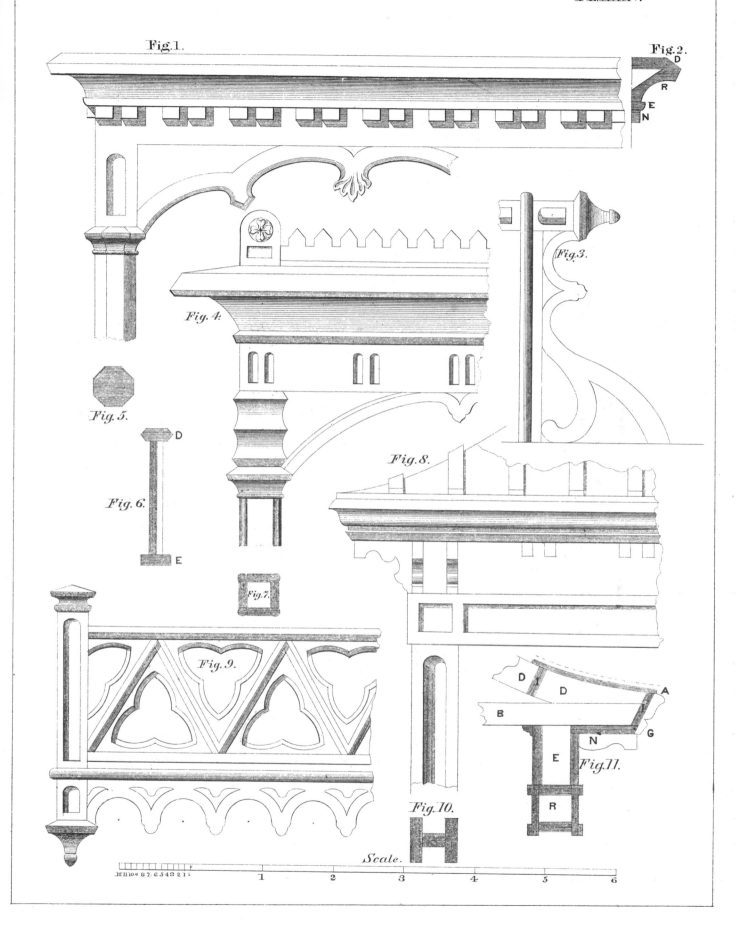

Fig.1.

Fig.2.

Fig.3.

Fig.4.

Fig.5.

Fig.6.

Fig.7.

Fig.8.

Fig.9.

Fig.10.

Fig.11.

Scale.

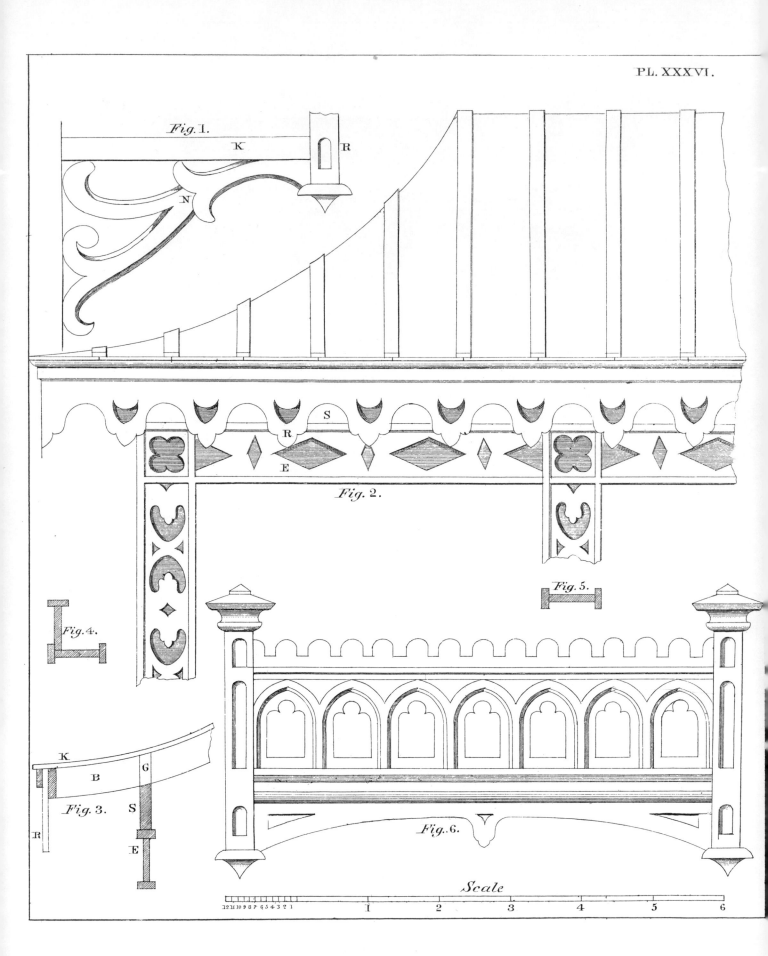

PL. XXXVI.

*Fig.*1.

K R

N

Fig. 2.

S

R

E

*Fig.*4.

Fig. 5.

K

B G

Fig. 3. S

R

E

Fig. 6.

Scale

12 11 10 9 8 7 6 5 4 3 2 1   1   2   3   4   5   6

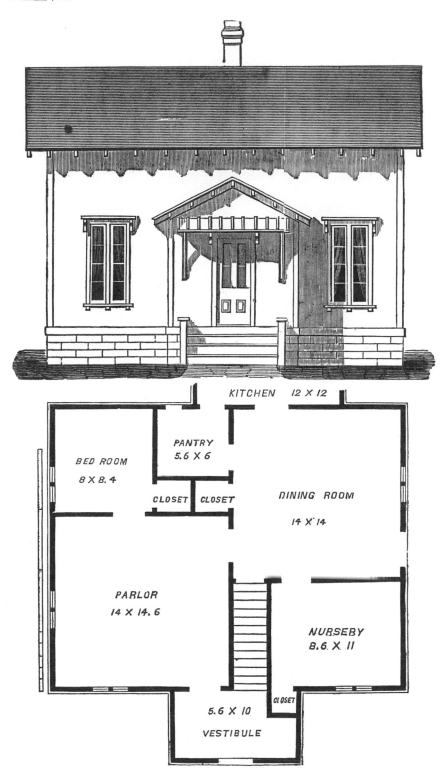

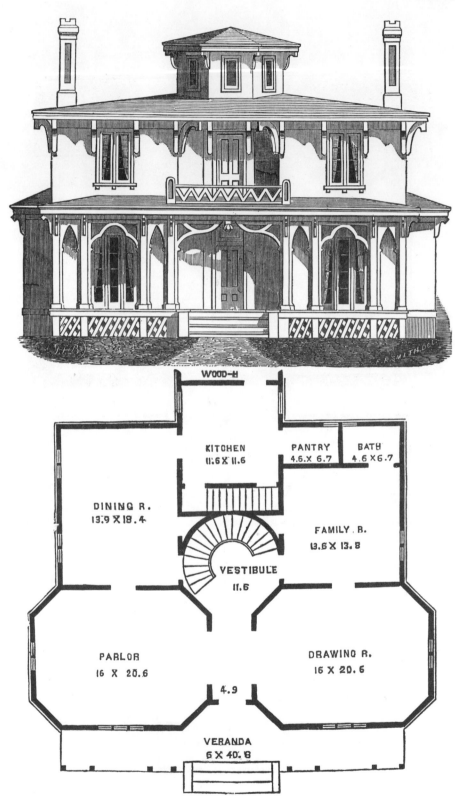

WOOD-H

KITCHEN
11.6 X 11.6

PANTRY
4.6 X 6.7

BATH
4.6 X 6.7

DINING R.
13.9 X 18.4

FAMILY R.
13.6 X 13.8

VESTIBULE
11.6

PARLOR
16 X 25.6

DRAWING R.
16 X 20.6

4.9

VERANDA
6 X 40.8

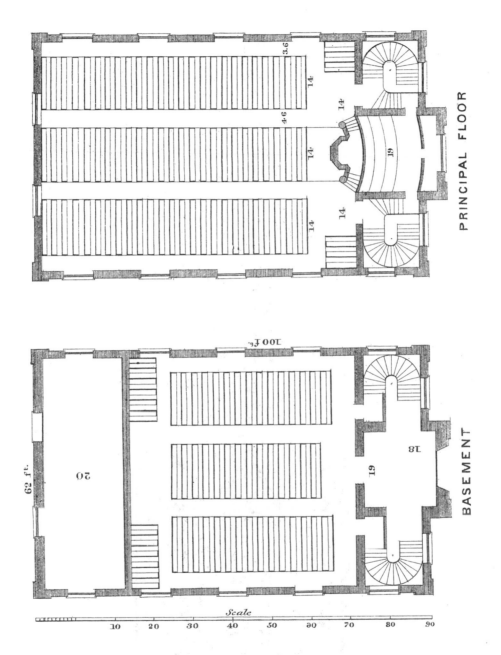

PRINCIPAL FLOOR

BASEMENT

Scale

10   20   30   40   50   60   70   80   90

5 10 20 30 40 50 60

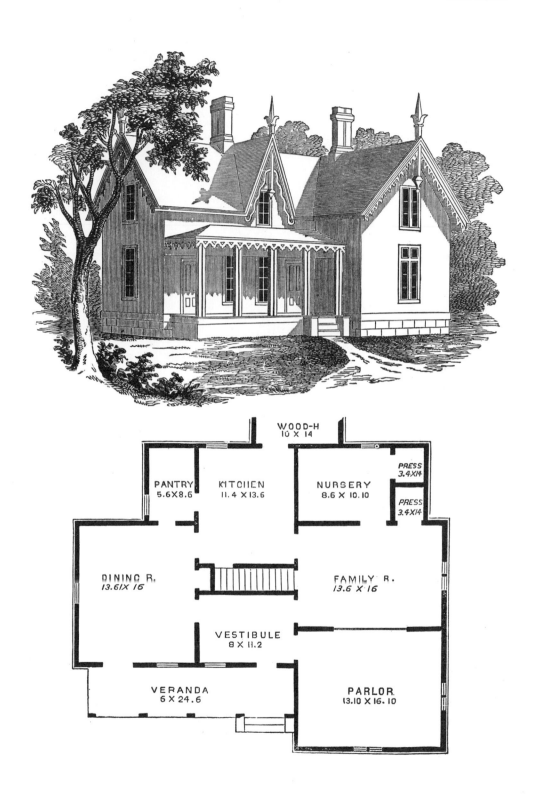

WOOD-H
10 X 14

PANTRY
5.6X8.6

KITCHEN
11.4 X 13.6

NURSERY
8.6 X 10.10

PRESS
3.4 X14

PRESS
3.4 X14

DINING R.
13.61X 16

FAMILY R.
13.6 X 16

VESTIBULE
8 X 11.2

VERANDA
6 X 24.6

PARLOR.
13.10 X 16. 10

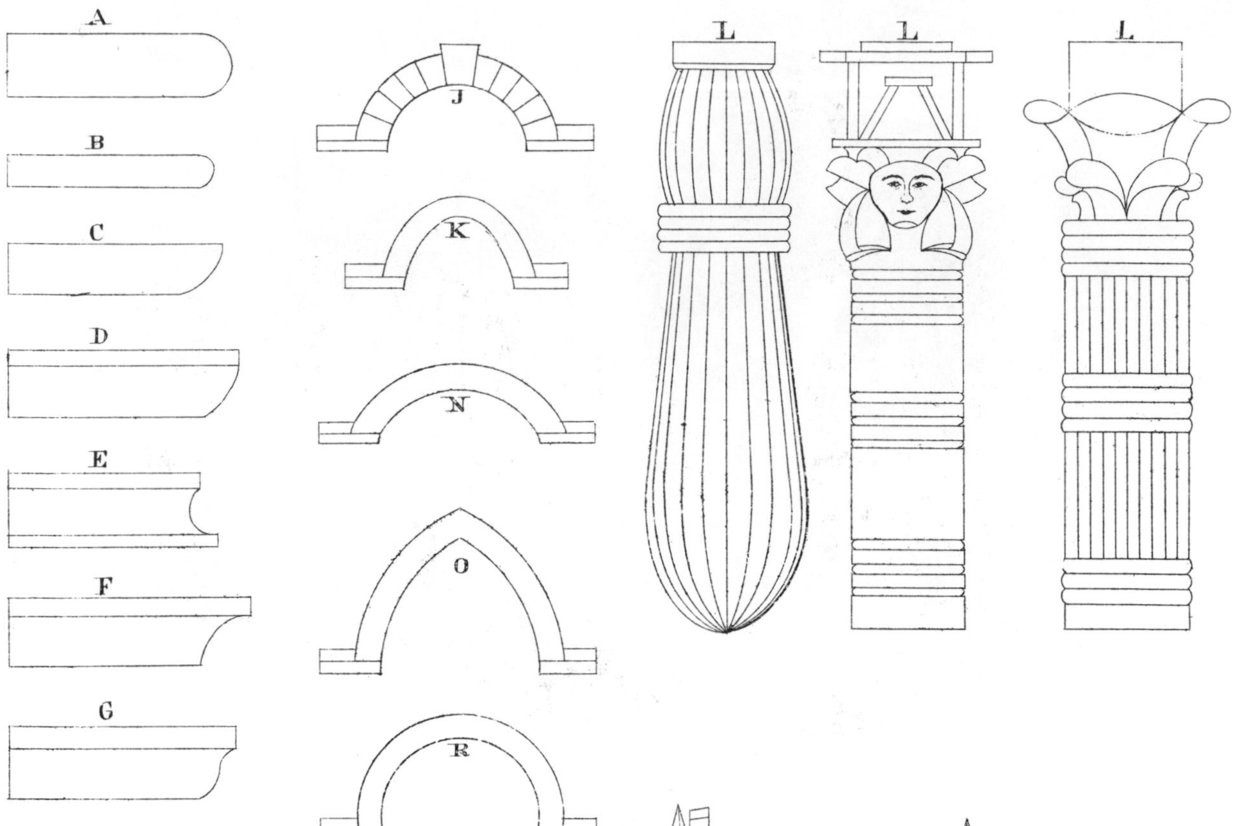

A

B

C

D

E

F

G

H

I

J

K

N

O

R

S

V

L

L

L

W

Y

X

P